"*Children of Hoarders* provides a clear and thoughtful path out of the pain, terror, and shame of loving a parent who hoards. Filled with practical suggestions to manage a multitude of problems that plague adult children with a parent who hoards, readers are certain to visit and revisit this resource and pass it on to other family members who are looking for a way to help someone they love who hoards and, as importantly, to help themselves."

—**Michael A. Tompkins**, PhD, cofounder of the San Francisco Bay Area Center for Cognitive Therapy; clinical professor at the University of California, Berkeley; and author of *Digging Out: Helping Your Loved One Manage Clutter, Hoarding, and Compulsive Acquiring*

"If you are growing up in fear of your doorbell ringing because your parent is a hoarder, then this book is for you. Children of hoarders need support as much as any other group struggling with an addicted family member."

—**Amy Doyle**, supervising producer of seasons one and two of TLC's *Hoarding: Buried Alive*

"Written by experts in the field of hoarding research, this information-packed manual for children of hoarders offers helpful strategies for minimizing the suffering that naturally accompanies watching someone you love suffer, as well as fascinating explanations for the roots of hoarding behavior. As a child of a hoarder, I highly recommend it."

—**Jessie Sholl**, author of *Dirty Secret: A Daughter Comes Clean About Her Mother's Compulsive Hoarding*

CHILDREN
of
HOARDERS

HOW TO MINIMIZE CONFLICT, REDUCE THE CLUTTER & IMPROVE YOUR RELATIONSHIP

FUGEN NEZIROGLU, PhD, ABBP
KATHARINE DONNELLY, PhD

NEW HARBINGER PUBLICATIONS, INC.

Publisher's Note

Distributed in Canada by Raincoast Books

Copyright © 2013 by Fugen Neziroglu and Katharine Donnelly
New Harbinger Publications, Inc.
5674 Shattuck Avenue
Oakland, CA 94609
www.newharbinger.com

Cover design by Sara Christian; Text design by Michele Waters-Kermes;
Acquired by Tesilya Hanauer; Edited by Will DeRooy

Library of Congress Cataloging-in-Publication Data

Neziroglu, Fugen A., 1951-
  Children of hoarders : how to minimize conflict, reduce the clutter, and improve your relationship / Fugen Neziroglu, PhD, ABBP, ABPP, and Katharine Donnelly, PhD.
    pages cm
  Includes bibliographical references.
  ISBN 978-1-60882-438-0 (pbk. : alk. paper) -- ISBN 978-1-60882-439-7 (pdf e-book) -- ISBN 978-1-60882-440-3 (epub) 1. Storage in the home. 2. Compulsive hoarding. 3. Obsessive-compulsive disorder. 4. Parent and child. I. Donnelly, Katharine. II. Title.
  TX309.N49 2013
  648'.8--dc23

                              2013033440

Printed in the United States of America

15   14   13

10   9   8   7   6   5   4   3   2   1   First printing

Contents

Acknowledgments

This book was inspired by our work with children of hoarders and our observation of the unique struggle that life as a child of a hoarder brings with it. Hoarding is one of the few disorders that spill out (literally and figuratively) on family and loved ones. While the psychological and practical consequences of hoarding are bad enough for hoarders themselves, children of hoarders often have no choice but to live like hoarders too, even if they do not share the disorder. The emotional turmoil that this causes is far reaching, affecting these children's psychological development as well as their social opportunities and ability to maintain proper hygiene.

We especially thank those individuals who shared their stories with us, contributing to the narratives in this book. Their assistance was invaluable in helping us to do justice to the experiences of children of hoarders, and to address their needs.

We also thank the researchers and clinicians who have contributed to the literature relating to hoarding and behavioral research. Randy Frost, PhD, and Gail Steketee, PhD, who have pioneered the work on hoarding, have inspired many others to research this disorder. We are grateful for all of those who have provided insight into hoarding through their research, without which we could not have compiled the recommendations in this book. Researchers in the area of acceptance-oriented treatments also made a vital contribution to the theoretical foundation of this book. The works of Steven Hayes, PhD, Kelly Wilson, PhD, and

Kurt Strosahl, PhD, contributed to many of the recommendations in this book, and the researchers deserve our gratitude.

We also acknowledge the people at New Harbinger Publications who worked relentlessly to help ready this book—specifically acquisitions manager Tesilya Hanauer, associate acquisitions editor Melissa Valentine, and freelance copyeditor Will DeRooy.

Finally, we acknowledge the support of our friends and family members.

INTRODUCTION

Children of Hoarders

I don't know what to do anymore. My mom is all alone in that house, and her things are basically swallowing her alive. Her disability makes it difficult for her to get to many areas of the house, and I worry every day that she'll fall as a result of the clutter. I constantly fear I'll get a phone call that she has been found dead in the home, but on the other hand I can't help but want to ignore the situation completely. The guilt that this causes me is overwhelming. Most of my family has stopped reaching out to her. She becomes more and more isolated every day, and because she refuses to do anything about the clutter and the squalor, there's no end in sight—no repair to the damage done to the relationships in our family. I feel almost constant guilt, shame, anger, resentment, and fear about the future. My own relationships have suffered as a result. Like I said, I don't know what to do to end this cycle.

—Joanne

Joanne's story illustrates the internal conflict that children of compulsive hoarders often grapple with. The gravity of the situation, coupled with feeling helpless and powerless to fix the problem, leads to an unworkable and immensely heartbreaking daily struggle. Given that you are reading this book, most likely this vicious cycle is all too familiar to you. Maybe as a child you were too ashamed to invite your friends to your house or did not have a space to call your own because of your parent's hoarding. Maybe you argue endlessly with your parent about the hoarding, or maybe you avoid the subject completely. No matter how long your parent has hoarded or how it has affected your life, the concepts we discuss in this book are likely to be helpful to you.

Following are some important concepts upon which the strategies we will recommend are based.

Your first responsibility is to yourself and your own well-being. You cannot be who you need to be for others if you are not first taking care of yourself. When you are dealing with a problem such as a parent who hoards, self-care is a necessity—though it is sometimes easier said than done.

Your control over your parent is limited. It is hard enough to change your own behavior, let alone someone else's. No matter how much you love someone; no matter how desperate or dangerous circumstances seem to you; no matter how much effort you put into getting someone to change, the scope of your influence is limited. Throughout this book, we will elaborate on the possibility that taking a step back or letting go of the reins a bit is often a more effective and less stressful approach.

You cannot bully or guilt your parent into changing. It is easy to get drawn into a power struggle with a hoarder, and hostile statements (e.g., "Clean up this mess or I've had it with you!") may seem necessary to make the hoarder realize the seriousness of the situation. Unfortunately, this often contributes to strife in the relationship, thereby undermining supportive or validating communication, and making it less likely that the hoarder will listen to your concerns about the conditions of the home. We will explore assertively setting boundaries with your parent who hoards as an alternative to making hostile statements or demands.

Accommodating your parent's hoarding is also unproductive. Family members of hoarders often default to behaviors that unwittingly enable hoarding (e.g., bringing take-out food to a hoarder when the hoarder's kitchen is too cluttered to be usable for food preparation). While such behaviors may seem natural and caring, they may actually make the hoarder more comfortable with continuing his dysfunctional habits. Obviously, there are many special considerations when deciding what to do or not do for your parent, especially where medical or safety issues are concerned. We will discuss these considerations. For the time being, it will suffice to say that accommodating a hoarder usually enables him or her to continue hoarding. Later, we will help you assess your possible contribution to this pattern and consider ways to change it.

Behaviorally, compulsive hoarding may resemble substance abuse and other impulse control disorders (e.g., pathological gambling and compulsive hair pulling). Like these other disorders, hoarding may be dangerous—even life-threatening—not only for the person with the problem, but also for the entire household. For these reasons, we will tap into the psychology of addiction as far as how family members might manage their approach to the hoarder's behaviors.

Your efforts to solve the problem are subject to the law of diminishing returns. This basically means that the more that you extend yourself, the less productive your efforts become. We will emphasize the use of mindful, tactful, and purposeful efforts rather than frantic, desperate, or pressured ones.

Your frustration and sadness about your parent's problem emerged out of a genuine desire to help your parent live a better life. The efforts that you have made on your parent's behalf— though they may have not always had the desired outcome—have come from an honest investment in your parent's well-being.

OUR OBJECTIVES

We hope to offer some solutions to those who have witnessed a parent's hoarding and tried in vain to turn things around. In the following chapters, you will find practical solutions for effectively communicating with your parent about the problem, as well as suggestions for coping with the emotional burden. In addition to learning about your role and responsibility in this process, you will have the chance to practice new, more effective ways of handling your parent's hoarding and dealing with your emotional responses to it. The approach we propose entails *acceptance* and *mindfulness*. Acceptance does not suggest that you should condone your parent's behavior or resign yourself to a life of unhappiness. Rather, acceptance involves dropping your struggle against unpleasant feelings, which will enable you to walk steadily through difficult situations and periods of chaos or uncertainty. We will explore *willingness* to have your current experience, and just let the present moment be what it is, while you—to the best of your ability—carry your life in the direction that you want it to go. Mindfulness, a focus on the present moment rather than the past or the future, can help you reduce your worries. Acceptance and mindfulness will be explored in greater detail starting in chapter 4.

Ultimately, this book is not about getting your parent to change, but about changing how you relate to the dysfunctional aspects of your parent's life. Even if you are currently estranged from your parent, or if your parent does not want help or is not even open to discussing the problem, you have authority over your own reactions, and you can set the stage to move your relationship with your parent in a healthier direction.

As you read this book, you will learn to:

- Use assertive and validating communication to discuss sensitive topics with your parent who hoards.

- Apply mindfulness and acceptance strategies to manage your emotions related to your parent's hoarding, helping you act assertively and effectively.

- Apply principles of assertive communication to confront your parent about the problem.

- Set boundaries and reclaim areas of the home.

- Navigate resources available to you and your parent.

- Resist an enabling role.

- Manage the estate of a hoarder who has passed away.

- Make your own well-being a priority and employ self-care strategies.

HOW TO USE THIS BOOK

Given that you are reading this book, you have probably tried everything you can think of to fix the problem of your parent's hoarding, without success. We understand that you did not ask to be in your present situation; you are not responsible for your parent's dysfunctional behavior patterns. We also understand that your parent's dysfunctional behavior patterns have had a profound impact on you, and that you need support. Ultimately, however, you have a choice: going forward, you can do things that will lead to more productive outcomes, both for yourself and for your parent, or you can do things that will result in further stagnation. We only ask that you examine your own behavior and entertain a new approach.

This book is meant to be both informational and interactive. The exercises are intended to allow you to put the concepts we discuss into practice. Some chapters elaborate on specialized topics such as cleaning up the home after the passing of a parent who hoards (chapter 10). Feel free to focus on the chapters that are most relevant to your specific situation, but consider the suggestions we make in all chapters as part of a unified approach: establishing boundaries, following through with consequences, and effectively and assertively communicating with family members about the problem.

As you read this book, you may try to establish some relationship with your parent outside of his or her hoarding, or you may find that you need to walk away and not look back. Whatever the choice, the feelings you will struggle with are not likely to be positive ones. Learning to acknowledge and accept these feelings, however, is important. And we will provide strategies for dealing with unpleasant emotions in the pages to come.

CHAPTER 1

Understanding Hoarding

THE PROBLEM UNDERLYING THE MESS

It is **very understandable** if you feel intense anger toward your parent who hoards for the position in which the hoarding has put you and the rest of your family. If you grew up with the shame, embarrassment, helplessness, inconvenience, and even unhealthiness that can accompany a parent's hoarding, or if your parent began hoarding later in life and you are struggling to understand why, it is likely that you have a hard time empathizing with your parent in this regard and comprehending the psychological dysfunction that underlies the compulsion to hoard. Resentment and frustration are common in this situation.

That said, you do not have to struggle alongside your parent. You are independent of your parent, and you have authority over your own response to what you observe. So while it is likely that you feel angry and resentful, you can choose to move forward with your own life while dealing with your parent deliberately and assertively. That your parent feels controlled by impulses to hoard doesn't mean that you need to be similarly controlled by your parent's behavior. We are suggesting not that you agree with your parent's behavior, but that you may benefit if you strive to understand it and forgive the hurt that you have felt as a result of it.

The first step in the process of recovery from the ways in which your parent's hoarding has affected you is to gain some insight into the problem. In this first chapter, we will elaborate on what hoarding is, what drives it, and how it is experienced by the hoarder. We hope that this exploration will help you understand how many hoarders feel when their "stuff" is touched, and what causes the sense of panic, desperation, and threat to their identities. Our aim is not to excuse hoarding behavior or say that it is not a serious problem, but rather to arm you with the understanding that will enable you to accept the situation for what it is and make deliberate changes in your relationship with your parent who hoards.

What is it like when you walk into your parent's house? Take a moment right now to imagine the scene. Visualize pulling into the driveway, opening the front door, greeting your parent, and so on. What thoughts and feelings typically arise on these occasions?

What problems come to your attention? What worries or fears come to mind when you think about the state of your parent's home? Maybe you feel ashamed, angry, or disgusted; maybe you worry that your parent will fall when navigating through a cluttered area; maybe you worry that the poor air quality is affecting your parent's health or your own—the negative effects of hoarding, both emotional and practical, are many. And while these effects might be similar across cases of hoarding, the causes of hoarding behavior are highly individual. Essentially, the *problem with the mess* relates to the health and safety issues, as well as the stigma associated with hoarding; but the *problem underlying the mess* may have enormous implications for the course and treatment of hoarding.

PRIMARY VS. SECONDARY HOARDING

In this chapter, we make a distinction between "primary" and "secondary" hoarding. These terms relate to both the cause of the behavior and how important the things being hoarded are to the hoarder. Secondary hoarders live with extreme clutter or squalor as a result of some other psychological or neurological condition, such as obsessive-compulsive disorder (OCD), obsessive-compulsive personality disorder (OCPD), or dementia, but they feel no particular attachment to the items that make up the clutter. While primary hoarding may also be the result of another disorder, the difference is that primary hoarders have strong feelings about or feel an emotional connection to the things they hoard. This is important because your parent's willingness to cooperate with your requests will vary based on the underlying cause of the hoarding behavior.

For example, people with dementia-related hoarding (secondary hoarders) are likely to continue to hoard if their behavior is not monitored, but hoarding is not the only manifestation of the problem; unsafe behaviors (e.g., taking medication improperly) are

11

evident in almost every aspect of their daily routine. These people may not hoard deliberately; rather, failure to get rid of garbage or keep their homes clean is an example of the many ways in which their functioning has declined as a result of neurological degeneration. But because those with dementia cannot function independently, they must yield when family members intervene. They are also unlikely to suffer extreme grief following a purge of things they hoarded. Primary hoarders, on the other hand, may function normally in all other areas of life; they may appear completely "together" in every way outside of their homes. But the emotional attachments that they form with the objects they hoard may be so strong that decluttering may represent an incredible loss, akin to bereavement. Primary hoarders may be more resistant to intervention, and they may truly grieve the loss of their items, making cleanup emotionally exhausting for everyone involved.

Diagnostic classification of hoarding behavior is ever evolving. Researchers in the field are always trying to better understand whether hoarding is rightly a symptom of other disorders or a disorder in itself, as well as what class of disorder it best fits into: OCD, impulse control disorder, or personality disorder. Below, we will explore the different manifestations of hoarding behavior as they relate to primary and secondary hoarding, and further on we will discuss the different reasons that primary hoarders cite for their behavior and what this means in terms of their difficulty getting rid of things. If you understand the type of hoarding your parent may have, you may find it easier to deal with.

DISORDERS RELATED TO HOARDING

Until recently, hoarding behavior was considered a subtype of OCD. However, one change in the recently published fifth edition of the American Psychiatric Association's *Diagnostic and Statistical Manual of Mental Disorders* is that hoarding is now defined as a disorder in its own right. However, it is fair to say that hoarding behavior is present in a number of psychological or neurological disorders. As you read over the various disorders below in which hoarding is present, see whether you can tell what type of hoarding behavior your parent has. It may be helpful to jot down some of the traits and behaviors you identify in your parent as you read. We will start with the traditional categorization of hoarding as a subtype of OCD.

Obsessive-Compulsive Disorder (OCD)

OCD is characterized by intrusive thoughts and an obsessive focus on unrealistic or inflated threats, with corresponding compulsive behaviors that are performed in an effort to minimize the sufferer's anxiety. People with OCD and people who hoard both demonstrate extreme indecisiveness. Both have anxious compulsions that can turn everyday activities (e.g., organizing or discarding materials) into laborious processes that they would rather avoid. Both are extremely sensitive to the question "What if…?" And both tend to be averse to taking risks. Hoarders frequently say that they do not want to discard an item in the event that it will be needed one day. This suggests that fear of deprivation, aversion to regret, skepticism about the unlikelihood of disastrous consequences actually occurring, and self-doubt all cause the hoarder to err on the side of caution.

As we mentioned, until recently, hoarding has been considered a subtype of OCD, but researchers also stress that it may be more distinct than other OCD subtypes. OCD subtypes such as compulsive checking, contamination phobia, and scrupulosity (i.e., dysfunctional focus on moral issues, and compulsive measures aimed at "being a good person") tend to be pervasive, touching upon many types of obsessions and compulsions, whereas hoarding usually stands alone (Olatunji et al. 2008). There is some evidence to suggest that the causes of OCD and the causes of hoarding are different. Still, a person with OCD may have either primary or secondary hoarding (or both), as illustrated in the following vignettes.

■ Molly: Primary Hoarding

Molly, a mother of two, demonstrated traditional obsessive-compulsive symptoms throughout much of her life. She developed hoarding behavior after the death of her husband when she was forty years old. She began collecting and saving toys and other such children's items, among other things that she believed might be useful at some point. By the time she was sixty-five, the basement, the living room, and all three bedrooms of her house were completely impassable. Her living room and kitchen featured characteristic *goat trails* (narrow passages through rooms full of clutter), and she slept on her couch—actually, on half of her couch—the only piece of furniture in her home not completely covered in clutter. The kitchen was generally unusable, and so she stored her food next to the couch where she slept.

Molly's obsessive thoughts related to the usefulness or sentimental value of each item that she owned. She was able to imagine a scenario in which she would need every item in her possession, and she did not recognize that her behaviors were dysfunctional. Molly would frequently become tearful when discussing items of sentimental value, particularly those connected to or belonging to her children or late husband.

■ Andrew: Secondary Hoarding

Throughout his adolescence, Andrew exhibited symptoms of OCD, which became more pronounced in his twenties. His symptoms predominantly involved contamination phobia, as well as compulsive checking. Specifically, he was very particular about which objects were okay to touch, and when "contaminated" he would engage in a lengthy and involved washing ritual. Furthermore, he felt the need to check every piece of trash before discarding it, carefully examining it to ensure that it did not contain anything valuable.

While he was able to live on his own and maintain employment, Andrew became overwhelmed by his OCD. As a result of his phobia, he would not touch certain "contaminated" areas of his home, contributing to its squalid conditions, and he would not sort through clutter or organize anything because the clutter also felt dirty and contaminated. The result was that the clutter just kept accumulating.

Although Andrew had difficulty throwing things away, which resembles hoarding, his difficulties were entirely explained by symptoms of other OCD subtypes. He felt no emotional attachment to objects, and he would have preferred a less cluttered residence, but sorting his possessions was so exhausting or anxiety-provoking due to his OCD that his home grew to resemble that of a primary hoarder.

Obsessive-Compulsive Personality Disorder (OCPD)

OCPD is characterized by extreme behavioral rigidity or inflexibility. People with OCPD adhere to a strict set of rules or restrictions, which they often try to force others to follow as well. They show obsessive preoccupation with certain topics in the same way that people with OCD do, and they also carry out compulsive behaviors in response to obsessions. The foremost difference between OCD and OCPD is that those with OCD are very distressed by the presence of obsessive or intrusive thoughts, while people with OCPD fully believe their thoughts; they do not necessarily see their lifestyle in a dysfunctional light. To put it another way, OCD bothers the person who is suffering with the disorder while OCPD does not, although OCPD may be distressing to those around the person: coworkers, employers, family members, and so on. Compulsive behaviors are less ritualistic and more enjoyable for people with OCPD than for people with OCD. Hoarding has been considered a very common symptom of OCPD and was once even included among the diagnostic criteria. The relationship between OCPD and hoarding is logical: many hoarders are defensive about their lifestyle, insisting that there is no problem with their hoarding behaviors. Furthermore, many hoarders are described as "stubborn" or "rigid" and have difficulty relinquishing control or delegating tasks.

■ Tim: Primary Hoarding Related to OCPD

Tim, a seventy-year-old married man, bought more books, magazines, and newspapers than he could read, reasoning that one day he would have time to read them. Yet he felt as though he could not afford to discard any reading material even after he had read it, in the event that it contained some information that might someday be useful to him. In addition to reading materials, Tim hoarded broken appliances, with the expectation that he would repair them one day.

Tim's wife wanted him to discard the things he hoarded, and because he had such difficulty complying, she was often very angry. Tim maintained that he saw no problem with his tendency to save, even though there were few usable areas of the home remaining—the rest was filled with "junk," as his wife called it. He was unable to recognize that his hoarding was a problem, and he insisted that his wife was the one with the problem, in that she could not see the potential value of the items he had saved throughout the years. He ended up going for treatment only at his wife's insistence.

Attention Deficit Disorder (ADD)

Does your parent have difficulty concentrating, focusing, and keeping track of or remembering things? If so, your parent may have attention deficit disorder (ADD). People who have ADD are disorganized and cannot prioritize. Their thoughts race. Their attention jumps around. In conversation they often interrupt, seem not to listen, or randomly change the subject. Because they are not focused, they often accomplish very little or leave things undone. Obviously not everyone with ADD hoards; however, hoarding can be a consequence of ADD when items accumulate in the home as a result of disorganization and a tendency to leave things undone. Impaired attention to fixing the mess leads to the clutter becoming overwhelming.

Dementia

Hoarding is very common among the elderly, specifically those with dementia. One study indicated that 15 percent of nursing home residents and 25 percent of elderly community dwellers demonstrated clinically significant hoarding behavior (Marx and

Cohen-Mansfield 2003). Many people in some phase of cognitive decline (related to dementia, for example) late in life exhibit hoarding behavior for the first time or show a worsening of preexisting hoarding behavior. For example, some people with OCD or OCPD who did not previously exhibit dysfunctional or dangerous hoarding behavior begin to do so after the start of a cognitive decline.

Hoarding behavior that develops after the onset of dementia is considered secondary hoarding. Hoarders with dementia are more likely to hoard garbage, a phenomenon referred to as *syllogomania*, which is dangerous to the health of everyone in the home. Although it is currently unclear whether hoarding among patients with dementia is brought on by the same causes as hoarding among those without dementia, we do know that areas of the brain often affected by neurodegenerative processes, specifically Alzheimer's disease, are associated with attention, memory, executive functioning/planning, and spatial reasoning (Wenk 2003). Hoarders have cognitive traits that reflect some of these same deficits, including indecisiveness, inattention, and executive functioning difficulties. Of course, these traits are mild compared to the extreme deficits that become evident among people with neurological degeneration. However, this overlap may help explain why hoarding tendencies sometimes arise under conditions that cause dementia.

■ Helen: Secondary Hoarding as a Symptom of Dementia

In her sixties, Helen developed a neurodegenerative disorder, resulting in symptoms of dementia, including an impaired ability to retain new information, as well as slurred speech, inability to organize, and difficulties of attention. Prior to the onset of these symptoms, Helen had not demonstrated any hoarding tendencies. Yet Helen's husband and children became increasingly concerned about her housekeeping behaviors. She left spoiled food in the refrigerator and had no hesitation in serving it up; she became angry if anyone tried to dispose of any household items; she seemed agitated if anything changed in her environment; and piles of items were cropping up all throughout the house. She wanted to sort the mail, for example, but it just piled up. She was unfazed by the presence of cockroaches and mold growth under these conditions. Furthermore, her formerly healthy love of animals turned into a fixation with stray cats in the neighborhood; she would leave exorbitant amounts of food out for the cats, leading many strays to take up residence on her property.

While Helen demonstrated many behaviors associated with both common hoarding (hoarding of objects) and animal hoarding (discussed later in this chapter), they came about only after the onset of a neurodegenerative disorder. Therefore, Helen's hoarding is an example of secondary hoarding.

Depression

Depression may also mimic hoarding. People who are experiencing severe symptoms of major depressive disorder (MDD) often neglect basic household responsibilities. This may result in squalor, dilapidation, inability to stay "on top of" bills and other paperwork, and more, which can easily give a visitor to the home the impression that the person is a hoarder. This type of behavior represents secondary hoarding, however, as the depressed person does not necessarily have any emotional attachment to the unpaid bill, for example.

■ Lily: Secondary Hoarding as a Symptom of Depression

Lily's primary psychological concern related to chronic major depressive episodes, which she had experienced since late adolescence. When Lily finally went for treatment, she was in her midforties and living alone. While Lily's home did not resemble the average hoarder's home in that it did not contain floor-to-ceiling or wall-to-wall clutter, it demonstrated the disuse, disrepair, and squalor frequently observed in the homes of hoarders. Dishes were piled up; overall conditions were unsanitary; and it was clear that responsibilities were being neglected all over the home. However, these conditions resulted from Lily's lack of motivation and loss of interest in enjoyable activities, as well as self-neglect related to major depression, rather than an emotional attachment to items in the home.

HOARDING AS AN IMPULSIVE AND COMPULSIVE DISORDER

Researchers have also viewed hoarding as an impulse control disorder, akin to pathological gambling, trichotillomania (hair plucking), or dermatillomania (skin picking; Hartl et al. 2005). The basic distinction between impulsive urges and compulsive urges relates to positive reinforcement (attaining something that is pleasant) versus negative reinforcement (escaping or avoiding something that is unpleasant).

Impulsive behaviors relate to sensation-seeking—in other words, pleasure—and while engaging in impulsive behaviors may also soothe discomfort, it is inherently pleasurable. *Acquiring* is considered impulsive; the hoarder feels an urge to acquire (shop, go to garage sales, shoplift, etc.) and derives intense pleasure from doing so or having done so. This is often followed by a period of shame about the episode.

On the other hand, compulsive behaviors allow the hoarder to avoid or escape unpleasant feelings. *Saving*, or *failing to discard*, is frequently considered compulsive; by hanging on to items, hoarders avoid possible regret or intense feelings of loss. "Savers" fear the consequence of losing valuable items, whereas "acquirers" seek out pleasurable opportunities to acquire new items.

A hoarder rarely fits neatly into either the impulsive or the compulsive category; rather, hoarding behavior is usually a mixed bag of avoidance and pursuit. But, in either case, the result is the same: an unmanageable mass of items and extreme defensiveness about the problematic behavior. Take a moment right now to think of your parent who hoards. What comes to mind? Do you think that your parent is avoiding anxiety and displeasure by not getting rid of things or rather feeling pleasure in the pursuit of purchasing? Does your mother, for example, often discuss her purchases or show them to you? If so, this would better indicate impulsive, rather than compulsive, motivation.

How the Primary Hoarder Sees the World

If your father is a primary hoarder, he is unable to let go of his belongings because he likely sees these items as extensions of himself; his possessions are akin to his identity or his essence. Although you may not understand how your parent can be so emotionally attached to so many possessions (especially if these possessions appear to have no value), think about belongings that you are attached to. Bring to mind three items that, while you have a sentimental attachment to them, are without objective value. Perhaps you have held on to a stuffed animal from when you were a child or carefully kept a picture that your daughter drew for you. If you are like most people, you probably have several boxes' worth of prized sentimental possessions. Imagine that these possessions are actually in boxes (if they are not already). And imagine how you would feel if your friends and family members were relentlessly trying to convince you to take those boxes and throw them indiscriminately into the garbage. Imagine how devastated and betrayed you would feel if you suddenly discovered that some or all of your prized possessions had been discarded without your consent by the very people who love you most of all. Now instead of a few boxes, think about feeling the same way about a whole house full of objects. In a sense, if your father is a primary hoarder, the terror that he feels at the thought of parting with his possessions is likely akin to the way you would feel if something very valuable was being yanked away from you. While for the average person, the idea of losing a valuable object—whether it has sentimental value, monetary value, or great usefulness—is upsetting, the psychological loss it represents for the primary hoarder, who has a much higher degree of attachment to objects, is profound. Some of you may feel that, while your father is terrified of parting with his possessions, he is not terrified of parting with you. You may believe that his "stuff" is more important to him than you yourself are, even when you've tried to make him happy for so long. These are legitimate feelings, and we will go into them later. For now, however, we want to introduce the common manifestations of primary hoarding, in the hopes that this will help you to better understand what you and your parent have gone through.

SUBTYPES

Object (aka "common") hoarding refers to the hoarding of items that the average person might find useful. Examples are clothing in good condition, housewares, office supplies, functioning electronics or appliances, shoes, and decorative items. Hoarders often have difficulty discarding such things because they perceive them to have both monetary value and usefulness. And sometimes this assessment is accurate. Especially for hoarders who acquire excessively, items they have hoarded might be completely new or unused. Of course, the cost of acquiring and hoarding usually outweighs the value of the items, but your parent's belief in the value of these things is a major obstacle to signing on for treatment. The idea of discarding an item that may be needed in the future is highly offensive to a hoarder because items that have value are not "trash" and should not be treated as such.

Sometimes objects being hoarded are objectively useless, such as garbage; or unsanitary, such as spoiled food. This behavior may be associated with *Diogenes syndrome*, which is described as severe self-neglect and is associated with domestic squalor. This type of hoarding is often observed among, but is not exclusive to, the elderly or people with dementia. Hoarding of garbage and other unsanitary materials usually arises when the hoarder is already overwhelmed by the conditions of a home full of clutter. When piles of items are accruing in all areas of the home, and the mess appears intractable, any cleaning efforts seem to be just "a drop in the bucket." Many hoarders eventually become desensitized to messy and unsanitary conditions (a phenomenon called "clutter blindness"), more or less neglecting all environmental hygiene.

Animal hoarding refers to owning an excessive number of animals. Can you think of anyone who may be an animal hoarder? Having more than two or three dogs or cats does not mean that you are an animal hoarder. An animal hoarder usually has forty or more animals, and dead, dying, or diseased animals are pretty common, found in 50 percent of cases (Patronek 1999). Animal hoarders demonstrate an incredibly strong emotional attachment to the animals under their "care." And while it may seem contradictory to an observer, in that animals being hoarded are often neglected and unhealthy, animal hoarders often see themselves as saviors to the animals that they house. Animal hoarding often indicates difficulties in interpersonal relationships, sometimes relating to traumatic experiences or guilt over a life decision. Animal hoarders frequently report a high level of loneliness and related anxiety and depression. Again, although your parent may not be an animal hoarder, there is very little difference in terms of the emotional attachment to the animals versus emotional attachment to possessions. Of course, we recognize that animals are alive and possessions are not, but a hoarder's attachment to either one is the same. The hoarder is connected to the life or object in the same way; it is a part of the hoarder.

A common irony among object and animal hoarders is that the things being hoarded are not individually appreciated. If your father hoards magazines, he would not notice if an issue from thirty years ago was missing from the stacks; if your mother hoards cats, she might not notice if a kitten from the latest litter passed away; yet the *idea* of losing it inspires desperation and panic and may threaten your parent's sense of identity. As the child of a hoarder, you do not need to understand how this contradiction is possible, just that the emotional reaction that results is usually genuine. It is not an "act," done to be manipulative or difficult; rather, the fear of loss is legitimate and intense.

Sentimental and Instrumental Hoarding

As we mentioned, compulsive acquiring may resemble an impulse control disorder, in that people who compulsively acquire experience an urge beforehand, experience great satisfaction during acquiring episodes, and may feel regret or shame afterward. But because they frequently report that they feel anxiety prior to acquiring (i.e., acquiring reduces their anxiety), these behaviors are also considered compulsive.

Of course, saving and acquiring go hand in hand. A primary hoarder's failure to discard excessive, unusable, or unsanitary items may arise due to either *sentimental saving* or *instrumental saving* tendencies, which we summarize below. Compulsive hoarding or acquiring for perceived aesthetic value of the items may also be considered among this category.

SENTIMENTAL SAVING

Items saved for sentimental reasons may include objects that belonged to loved ones or anything that reminds the hoarder of important people or events in her life. Examples are newspapers from a time for which the hoarder feels nostalgic, clothing that was worn by the hoarder's deceased mother, or the hoarder's child's stuffed animals or pictures. The hoarder saves items in order to tap into memories and feelings about meaningful people or time periods. The hoarder may fear that if these items are lost or discarded, access to the memories may also be lost, a prospect that is unacceptable. People who hoard for this reason often indicate that items feel like "a part of" them; that in some way, without the sentimental items, they would somehow be less than whole. This is crucial in understanding primary hoarding for sentimental reasons; the prospect of being separated from the items being hoarded threatens the hoarder's very identity. If your mother, for example, exhibits these thoughts or behaviors, she may feel very connected to her possessions; to her, they may represent an inextricable aspect of her identity. Although you may think that it is a problem of hygiene and see the need for a cleanup, think twice. Cleanups can be very traumatic, and we have seen some cleanups lead hoarders to attempt suicide. If you try a forced cleanup, your parent will feel betrayed and will grieve the loss of the items, possibly leading to depression and hopelessness.

INSTRUMENTAL SAVING

Instrumental saving relates to the belief that the items being hoarded have a use. If you think about it, most seemingly useless items may be considered useful in some way. For example, empty yogurt containers may be containers for other things, broken objects may have decorative or artistic value, old clothes may be used as cleaning rags, or old newspapers may be used as wrapping paper. The potential uses for seemingly useless objects are endless, and the problem with this line of reasoning is that most hoarders will acquire far too many items to be able to put them all to use (maybe one yogurt container will be used to hold paper clips, but if you have four hundred yogurt containers, the likelihood of finding a purpose for all of them is slim, especially if you cannot find them amid all the other things you are hoarding). Similarly, the perceived usefulness of items may also apply to reading material. As in Tim's case above, a hoarder might save endless stacks of newspapers, magazines, and books, believing that one day a piece of information contained in these resources may be needed. Furthermore, instrumental hoarders often believe that their items have inherent worth or value, and that should they ever decide to sell them the items would generate a substantial income. Hoarders often overestimate the value of their items; and, given the typical conditions of a hoarder's home, the value of many items can be compromised by rodent or insect infestations, mold or mildew contamination, and so on. However, for many hoarders, as long as they can conceive a use for an item, discarding it is unacceptable.

At this point, you may have formulated some hypotheses about what type of hoarder your parent is. The next step is to ask yourself the questions below. The goal here is to bring to light why your parent hoards, and while this may not change your feelings or your course of action, it is our belief that in this case it is better to have insight into what is causing the problem.

> Was hoarding the first thing that you noticed was wrong? If not, what was the first thing you noticed that indicated that there was a problem?
>
> If a loss of cognitive functioning, depression, or attention difficulties, for example, preceded the cluttered conditions, your parent's hoarding might better be explained as a symptom of another disorder. If your parent always had OCD symptoms but developed hoarding behavior later on in life, an OCD spectrum disorder might also explain the hoarding.

What rationale does your parent give you as far as why items are saved?

In this rationale, do you discern evidence of instrumental saving? Sentimental saving?

What types of objects does your parent save? Does your parent seem to think that these objects are useful or important in some way? Or is the mess mostly garbage and other things that have simply piled up over the months or years?

If only garbage is being saved, and your parent does not seem overly attached to it, the hoarding behavior may be a symptom of a degenerative process.

Does your parent become noticeably distressed when the subject of getting rid of things arises? Does your parent ever express any feelings such as "If I get rid of (my late husband's) old razors, then I might lose touch with him"?

If so, this sounds a lot like primary hoarding.

SUMMARY

In this chapter, we distinguished primary hoarding from secondary hoarding: primary hoarders purposefully hoard for emotional reasons, such as sentimental attachment to objects, overidentification with objects, and a perception of inherent value and usefulness in seemingly useless objects. We also explored other reasons for hoarding behavior, specifically secondary hoarding. We summarized conditions associated with both primary and secondary hoarding, including obsessive-compulsive disorder (OCD), obsessive-compulsive personality disorder (OCPD), attention deficit disorder (ADD), dementia, depression, and impulse control disorders. We described subtypes of hoarding (animal and object), and we explored manifestations of hoarding (acquiring versus saving of objects), with emphasis on how hoarders think and feel about the objects that they accumulate.

The chapters that follow will begin to unpack the task of learning to cope with the unpleasant feelings that accompany your situation. It is likely that at this juncture you are feeling a bit hopeless or overwhelmed. A lesson that we are going to reinforce as we go along is that the antidote to chronic worry is present-moment focus, or *mindfulness*. As we proceed, we will reinforce the importance of bringing your attention to what is right in front of you (reading each new word right now, for example), rather than becoming fixated on a problem that lies somewhere in your past or somewhere in your future. The application of mindfulness to your predicament will be a central focus of this book. And as we proceed, we will illustrate the simultaneous simplicity and difficulty of this task.

CHAPTER 2

How Your Parent's Hoarding Affects You

Hoarding creates obvious health and safety issues, and it is well known that having a family member who hoards is burdensome and emotionally taxing. Because parents are the most important figures in children's lives—responsible for their health, safety, and emotional well-being—and because children are for the most part powerless to improve their circumstances, the emotional impact is greatest for children of hoarders.

EMOTIONAL HEALTH ISSUES

Whether you never felt properly nurtured, felt robbed of a "normal childhood," or suddenly had to jump into an authoritative role as an adult because of your parent's hoarding, the emotional consequences your parent's hoarding has had for you have no doubt been far reaching. What follows is one person's account of growing up in a home full of clutter that illustrates how hoarding affects children's lives into adulthood.

> *My mom has always hoarded, as far back as I can remember.*
> *She was always extremely sensitive about what items were*
> *discarded, and we knew not to "mess with Mom's piles."*
> *If anyone ever tried to clean up in the house, it was like*
> *World War III. We eventually backed off and gave her control*
> *of the house. Ultimately, she used the whole house to store her*
> *hoarded items, including my room. I remember when I was*
> *young, my friends would complain to me about how their*
> *mothers were bothering them to clean up their rooms, while*
> *I wished that keeping my room clean was even possible.*
> *No one in my life knew what I was coming home to. I never*
> *had friends over, and everyone in my family was extremely*
> *secretive about the conditions of my home. I don't really think*
> *of these early years as a childhood. I remember so much*

shame, confusion, and neglect. I moved out at twenty years old, and my parents later divorced. Since then, my mother's hoarding has accelerated, and the conditions of her house have become totally unlivable. Now I'm not only resentful of my childhood, I'm worried about my mom's future. I have grown from a child without nurturing to an adult with a burden. What's worse is that I see no solution to this situation, and therefore I see no end to the emotional suffering.

Exercise: Examine Your Timeline

Think for a moment how you felt about your parent's hoarding over the course of your life—first as a child, then as an adolescent, then as an adult. In a notebook or on a separate sheet of paper, answer the following questions with attention to how you felt about your parent's hoarding at these three stages in your life.

1. What was your biggest obstacle to living a "normal" life?

2. How did you handle it?

3. How did you regularly feel (angry, sad, resentful)?

4. What did you think about your parent's hoarding?

Do you notice any differences across your timeline? Did you behave differently at different ages? Did you think differently about your parent's hoarding? Obviously, if your parent's hoarding behavior developed later in life, your answers to these questions will reflect this. However, even if your parent's hoarding was not an issue early on, if you're like most children of parents who hoard, you can likely see that there were hints or warning signs of the current situation even then. When did you first notice feelings of shame about the conditions of your parent's home? Looking at your answers to the above questions, consider how your psychological well-being, as well as your approach to your parent's hoarding, has changed over the years. How has your emotional development been affected by your parent's hoarding? And how has this impact morphed over the years?

Below, we will explore common psychological experiences of children of hoarders.

Burden and Distress

Much has been written about the phenomenon of *caregiver burden*. This is a term that is used to describe a wide range of experiences that people endure when they are in a position requiring them to provide emotional or practical care for another person.

When a loved one is diagnosed with a psychological disorder, caregiver burden is associated with interpersonal conflict and chronic worry (Magne-Ingvar and Öjehagen 2005), as well as increased anxiety, depression, and coping failure (Boye et al. 2001). Peggy MacGregor (1994) of the Children's Hospital of Philadelphia identified many areas of life that are disrupted when a loved one is diagnosed with a mental illness, including finances, privacy, normal family activities, pleasures, and freedoms. Caregivers also may suffer loss of self-esteem, loss of sense of competence, loss of sense of control, loss of pleasure in the loved one's accomplishments, loss of hope, loss of sense of security, and loss of ability to plan for the future. Although the studies mentioned above relate to caregiving for a wide variety of psychological issues, it stands to reason that family members of hoarders would experience similar devastation.

The impact of parental hoarding on children's development is gaining interest among researchers as a subject of study. In the coming years, we will no doubt see more attention paid to the experiences that you are already all too familiar with. For now, research on the social and emotional effects of hoarding on children, specifically, is scant; however, there are studies on the impact of other psychological disorders on family members, including children. Marlene Cooper (1996) surveyed family members (parents, spouses, children, siblings, and fiancés) of people with obsessive-compulsive disorder (OCD) and found that many of these family members experienced depression, perhaps due to the great stress and concern for their loved ones that they reported, and some had even attempted suicide. Thirty-two percent of the family members who responded to the survey were concerned with managing their own anger; 25 percent reported "envy of 'normal' families"; nearly 25 percent reported feelings of "mourning"; and 12 percent were concerned about the potential for their loved ones to experience serious harm.

Exercise: Examine Your Worry

Think for a moment about what exactly your worries are surrounding your parent's hoarding and jot them in a notebook or on a separate sheet of paper. What do you think may possibly happen to your parent? Are you mourning the loss of your relationship with your parent, worrying that your relationship will never be repaired? Or have you ever thought of your sadness as mourning for what you have *never* had? Do you worry that you will never be able to have a meaningful relationship with your parent now that the clutter stands between you and your parent, both literally and figuratively? Do you worry that if you now assert your need for distance from the situation you will be estranged from your parent, leaving him to his own devices? Let yourself really consider the question: what awful consequence do you fear? And how does this fear affect you on a day-to-day basis?

Other researchers (Ramos-Cerqueira et al. 2008) found similar results: depression, worry, and anxiety all tend to increase when a loved one is diagnosed with a psychological disorder. Family members are more likely to report feeling anxious or depressed, as well as more likely to report physical complaints. Perhaps you have suffered such effects yourself.

One study specifically examined the social and emotional effects of hoarding on family members (Tolin et al. 2008). The researchers asked family members of hoarders a few questions about the level of distress they experienced as a result of the hoarding. What they found is that among children of hoarders, the younger they were when the hoarding began, the more unhappy, more distressed, and overall less well adjusted they were. Children of hoarders indicated that they had difficulty making friends, were embarrassed to have people over to the house, and argued a lot with their parents. Interestingly, however, siblings of hoarders did not experience the same level of resentment and distress. This supports our personal observations that children of hoarders are more affected than other family members of hoarders.

Children living in a home full of clutter might feel incredible internal conflict when wondering what to do about the situation. The conditions of the home might represent a very shameful subject that all family members who are affected attempt to ignore or turn a blind eye to, much as with alcohol or drug addiction in some families. There may be an implicit concern that if the conditions of the home were openly discussed, the authorities might need to get involved. Neighbors might be judged more likely to complain about the dilapidated appearance of the home and school personnel more likely to report that a child is living in unsafe or unsanitary conditions; therefore, children and other family members are often urged to keep details of the conditions of the home a secret from friends, classmates, school officials, and others. This may have led you and other children of hoarders to experience shame and embarrassment, as well as fear of the legal implications if authorities inspected your parent's home. Furthermore, fear of being the one responsible for causing uproar in your parent's life, and the family as a whole, may have led you to incredible fear of the guilt that carelessness with this secret might cause. It is easy to see how the long-term effects on children may include intense inhibition and trepidation, emotional distance in outside relationships, and chronic anxiety.

The Pendulum Swings Both Ways

Understandably, children of hoarders often do not have the healthiest relationship with their own possessions. Observation of your parent's hoarding may have created in you the impulse to hoard as well; conversely, you may be so repulsed by hoarding that you have taken the opposite approach, discarding everything that is not immediately useful. If you do not live with your parent, perhaps you see a little clutter in your home as the beginning of a slippery slope and wish to clean it up immediately. On the other hand, you may find it challenging to maintain a clean and organized home because you never learned habits of good housekeeping from your parent. In the following chapters, we will explore what may be your own dysfunctional behaviors toward objects and introduce a compromise between the two extremes of excessive clutter and excessive cleanliness, if these are things you're struggling with. Of course, some of you have average housekeeping practices and normal attachments to personal belongings.

Your Experience

Above, we summarized research findings regarding how hoarding and other psychological disorders affect family members of those afflicted. Many of the experiences these family members described probably resonate with you. But you also probably do not need scientific verification to know that your parent's hoarding has affected your functioning. It is important that you give yourself the opportunity to take stock of how your parent's hoarding has interfered with your functioning. The following exercise is intended to distill some of the concrete ways in which you have been affected by your parent's hoarding. (In the next chapter, you will refer to your responses to this exercise to help you compose a letter.)

Exercise: Assess Your Experience

The following questions are meant to help you consider all the different ways that your parent's hoarding may have affected you. Answer all that apply to your situation. Write your answers in a notebook or on a separate sheet of paper.

1. What about your home or your parent's hoarding were you most ashamed of when you were growing up? How did this shame affect your feelings and beliefs about yourself?

2. How did your parent's hoarding affect your social life as a child? If you kept information about your parent's hoarding from friends, what kinds of lies did you have to tell?

3. Describe your relationship with your parent when you were a child. Was there a lot of conflict in the house?

4. What experiences were you robbed of as a result of your parent's hoarding?

5. As an adult, what do you and your family miss out on as a result of your parent's hoarding?

6. What are the most disastrous scenarios that you can conjure, as far as outcomes of your parent's hoarding?

7. How much time do you spend worrying or ruminating (recycling the same thoughts endlessly) about the mess your parent lives in?

8. How is your parent's hoarding currently affecting your relationship with your parent?

9. How is your parent's hoarding affecting your relationship with your other family members?

Your answers to the questions in the exercise above represent the reality of your parent's hoarding and its tragic consequences. Your feelings about these experiences are valid, and they need to be acknowledged, both by you and by your parent who hoards. In the following chapter, we will explore how to assertively discuss your parent's hoarding and your feelings about it with your parent. The goal of engaging in a dialogue with your parent who hoards is not necessarily to bring about change, but rather to begin the process of healing from the emotional impact that your parent's behavior has had on you.

PHYSICAL HEALTH AND SAFETY ISSUES

Now that we have looked at the psychological impact, we want you to think about the possible physical impact your parent's hoarding has had on you, more specifically the health and safety aspects. Few psychological disorders force loved ones to experience the consequences of a dysfunctional lifestyle as fully as hoarding does. Anyone who lives *with* a hoarder must live *like* a hoarder, by default. Even if nowadays you only visit your parent's home, for as long as you are there you must suffer the same health and safety consequences of hoarding as your parent.

Unsanitary Conditions

If your childhood home was always full of clutter, we are sure that you know that it was not the most sanitary place. Think about what it was like in the house in which you grew up. Was it difficult to get things out of the refrigerator because it was surrounded by piles? Was the sink full of dirty dishes, if you could even get to it through the clutter? Do you remember being afraid at times that the food you ate might be unsafe because it was past its expiration date? Had your mother or father lost the motivation to clean because the mess was too far gone? It is not surprising if as a child you had a lot of allergies or were often sick but did not know why, because under such conditions, the potential causes of illness are many.

PESTS

When things begin to pile up in a hoarder's home, it becomes harder to maintain sanitary conditions, especially in areas of the home in which perishables and other attractive treats for pests are stored. Because it is so hard to get through the piles to clean up the dirt and detritus, to dispose of the garbage, and to get rid of the expired food, a hoarder's home is fertile ground for unwanted guests. Both insect and other animal infestations, including mice, rats, cockroaches, ants, flies, spiders, and bedbugs, are common in the homes of hoarders. Depending on when your parent's hoarding became really bad, you may have been affected, slightly or enormously, by the presence of bugs and other vermin. Perhaps having pests around was the only life you had ever known, or you eventually got used to it.

Aside from the nuisance factor of an infestation, certain illnesses are associated with specific pests. Rodent and insect infestations may lead to salmonellosis in humans, an infection causing severe abdominal discomfort, vomiting, and diarrhea. Other diseases associated with rodent infestation include leptospirosis and hantavirus pulmonary syndrome. Allergies to animal and insect waste can cause extreme agitation when an infestation is present. Respiratory allergies can result in asthma, especially in young children.

PETS

Even if your parent was never an animal hoarder, the consequences of having just one or two pets in a home full of clutter can be disastrous. No one can argue that normally pets can bring joy to a home and even help people with certain illnesses; however, because hoarders frequently neglect basic cleanliness in the home or cannot access all areas to clean up after pets, the pet waste that accumulates can be a health hazard. For example, cats prefer to relieve themselves in a litter box, but if the litter box is not cleaned frequently, cats may choose a different or even multiple locations to "do their business"; and, in a home full of items being hoarded, most areas that are accessible to a cat are not accessible to a human. So the waste is never removed.

If animals themselves are being hoarded, the accumulated animal waste can be exponentially worse. Animal hoarding also increases the risk of rodent and insect infestation. And, in addition to the adverse health effects of infestation described above, animal hoarding increases the chances of contracting rabies, cat scratch disease, toxoplasmosis, and staph infections, among many other health problems and diseases. Oftentimes in cases of animal hoarding, diseased, dying, or dead animals are not properly cared for or disposed of, contributing to the overall squalor and unsanitary conditions of the home. Finally, the levels of ammonia (a pungent gas present in animal waste) in the house of an animal hoarder often exceed what is considered to be the healthy limit. Concentrated ammonia is potentially dangerous in unventilated areas, and can lead to respiratory distress or failure.

DUST AND MOLD

Do you remember having difficulty breathing in the house you grew up in? Did the house smell different than your friends' homes or other places you visited? If so, it may have been due to a preponderance of dust and mold. Both dust and mold may exacerbate or cause respiratory conditions, such as asthma and respiratory allergies. Just as is the case with ammonia levels in the home, poor ventilation due to the clutter and obstructed windows and doors intensifies the negative health effects of excessive dust and mold. Similarly, toxic mold, which is associated with some potentially life-threatening conditions, may be found within a home full of clutter. Certain types of mold contain *mycotoxins* (toxic chemicals produced by fungi in order to weaken the host). Depending on the strain of mold, the concentration of mold spores in an area, and the vulnerability of the person exposed to it, toxic mold can damage the lymphatic system, inhibit functioning of the immune system, and cause damage to the central nervous system.

OTHER ISSUES

Hoarders' homes are often associated with basic environmental squalor. Areas of the house that are generally affected include any room where food is stored and subsequently spoils, as well as bathrooms, areas where animals eliminate, and any plumbing area. Domestic squalor creates unsanitary conditions, which may lead to a variety of additional health issues such as dysentery, parasitic infections, and bacterial infections, among many others.

Loss of Accessibility

As the child of a hoarder, when you were growing up you may not have realized all the safety concerns related to the kind of environment in which you were forced to live. Now as an adult, you might be worried about the safety of your parent who hoards. You may also want to keep your children (or future children) safe. We know that for the elderly or the disabled, loss of accessibility of living spaces creates a potential for serious injury. Hoarders often create goat trails that allow them to get from one area of the home to another. Because these paths are narrow, they are difficult to navigate. Also, goat trails are often forged through tall stacks of possessions, and these stacks are generally unstable. Should one of these stacks topple, injury may result. Loss of accessibility also causes significant disruption to quality of life, which we will explore in greater detail below.

Fire Safety Issues

Whether you were aware of them or not as a child, you probably know now that hoarding creates many fire safety concerns. When a home is full of clutter, it is more vulnerable to the ignition of a fire; it increases the likelihood that a minor fire will turn into a major house fire; it makes it much more difficult for firefighters to extinguish the fire; and it decreases the likelihood that firefighters will be able to reach and rescue people trapped inside the home.

Hoarders' homes tend to have many issues related to disrepair, including electrical issues. Because hoarders tend to be ashamed of and secretive about their living conditions, they frequently avoid having repairmen and other outsiders enter their homes. Any areas of the home containing electrical damage are often inaccessible anyway due to the mess, and so repairs cannot be made if the hoarder never clears the clutter around damaged wiring. Damaged wiring may cause short-circuiting, and the sparks that result could start a fire. Old or damaged wires may also become very hot; if a wire becomes hot enough, this can also result in a fire. In addition, hoarders unfortunately tend to accumulate flammable items—piles of newspapers, magazines, books, and garbage are essentially kindling. And even beyond these obviously flammable items, the sheer volume of material in a hoarder's home increases its *fireload* (the amount of combustible material contained in a structure). Generally speaking, the greater the fireload, the more severe a house fire will be, and the more difficult it will be for firefighters to extinguish.

Furthermore, because smoke detectors in hoarders' homes are frequently nonworking and neglected, inhabitants may not be alerted to the presence of a fire right away. This is something most hoarders do not think about. Once the inhabitants are aware of the fire, clutter that blocks passageways might prevent them from safely exiting the home. When the blaze comes to the attention of the local fire department, firefighters will respond and do their best to prevent human casualty. However, we have been told by many fire departments that they take special precautions when entering the home of a hoarder because it is so dangerous to do so in a fire, and they will often opt to fight the fire only from the relative safety of the outside of the home. If they do enter the home, they may not be able to rescue anyone trapped inside, because of the obstacles the clutter presents to reaching them and exiting the home safely. Again, you were probably not aware of these myriad safety concerns as a child, and perhaps you have not given much thought to the risk of fire in the home. However, these are things to discuss with your parent. In future chapters, we will discuss techniques for talking to your parent about these troubling health and safety issues, as well as other topics that may be upsetting for you.

Loss of Structural Integrity

Depending on how long your parent has been hoarding, the house may be ready to collapse. A home piled high with possessions may simply be structurally unsafe. The weight of materials being hoarded may put stress on weight-bearing supports within the home and cause the whole thing to come tumbling down one day. Many times, rotting is evident in the foundation of a hoarder's home. Of course, think back to issues pertaining to disrepair in the house. If an area of the home needing repair is inaccessible, other problems may result. Over time, a simple leak, for example, may wreak havoc on the house. If a leaky roof causes water damage to a wall within the home, and the wall is inaccessible because of the clutter, the wood supports in the wall may begin to deteriorate. Affected areas may become vulnerable to infestation by insects that are attracted to moisture, such as carpenter ants. Thinking about it now, do you think you were safe in the house as a child? Is your parent who hoards safe now?

QUALITY-OF-LIFE ISSUES

Beyond health and safety concerns, hoarding conditions can lead to serious disruption to quality of life for everyone in the home. *Quality of life* relates to satisfaction in various areas of your life—your family, your leisure activities, your work or school, and so on. A good quality of life means that you are pretty satisfied in most areas, with a good balance of activities (e.g., in your work life versus your home life). People who live in a home full of clutter are forced to compromise their quality of life in many ways. Your parent's hoarding probably led to a poor quality of life when it came to family entertainment in the home (e.g., inviting people over, celebrating holidays, watching TV, and relaxing) and ease of daily living (e.g., having working appliances, heating or air conditioning, and functional bathrooms) and in many other ways that we will discuss below. In subsequent chapters, we will explore ways in which you can empower yourself and improve your overall quality of life.

Loss of Functional Living Space

There are many ways in which functional space can be lost when people hoard objects or animals. We will list some common ones, but no doubt you can think of others from your experience. Many children of hoarders never bathed in a tub, put their clothes away in a closet, stored their books on a bookshelf, or had an area in which to play, because all these places were packed with items their parent was hoarding. They never ate home-cooked meals because the oven was used for storage rather than cooking; the range had dirty dishes on it; and the kitchen countertops were piled with objects. Hoarders may try to keep their clutter limited to their own personal areas within the home, but it almost always extends into communal areas. When a bathroom is too full of clutter to be used for grooming and washing anymore, family members' hygiene might suffer. When a living room is full of clutter, the family has no communal social area. Essentially, when one family member is a hoarder, all normal household activities are either impeded or impossible.

When the clutter spills into your personal areas within the home, you are likely to feel even more violated by your parent's hoarding behaviors. It is very common for hoarders to eventually store hoarded items in all areas of the home, including other family members' designated territories. This is disruptive to children of hoarders at each developmental stage. Young children deserve a space to play and learn. Adolescent children need their own space, both to organize and decorate it in line with their emerging identities, and to study for and succeed in school. Adult children are entitled to privacy and freedoms. The good news is that, if you are currently living with your parent who hoards, in the following chapters, we will discuss how you can reclaim functional living space for yourself.

Loss of Social Life

Because hoarding often disrupts the use of communal areas within the home, those who live in such a home often miss out on social opportunities. For example, growing up you may not have been able to have playdates at your house. You may not have been able to host a sleepover. When you were older, you may not have been able to invite your boyfriend or girlfriend over to meet your parents. At each stage of your life, you probably felt as though you were missing out on what others were enjoying.

Yet dwelling on the experiences you have lost is not going to make you feel better. Instead, accept that you have control over your life *now* and can negotiate your relationship with your parent, as we will show you. Going forward, try to think of what you want from your parent now, not of what you did not get in the past.

Legal and Ethical Issues

Many of the lifestyle concerns described above pose legal and ethical issues. Social services may take action to remove a child from the home if hoarding creates potentially dangerous conditions for the child. Many professionals who work with children, such as school officials, psychologists, and social workers, are "mandated reporters." This means that they are legally required to inform social services if they believe that a child may be in any kind of serious danger. Determining what is "dangerous" can be complicated and nuanced, and mandated reporters do not always know what problems they are looking for. However, once social services is notified, an investigation ensues, and officials visit the premises to assess potential dangers. Severe hoarding conditions do represent legitimate dangers for children, for all of the reasons discussed above. Furthermore, in many communities, known hoarders are targeted by the local government, often resulting in eviction and/or repair of the home at the owner's expense. We know very well that children of hoarders who are old enough to know that the state of the home is a problem often do not report the conditions of their home because they are afraid of what will happen to their parents if the authorities intervene, because they are afraid that they will be taken to a foster home, or because they are ashamed of their homes and their parents. As we discussed earlier, this internal conflict may cause a great deal of stress for children.

SUMMARY

While hoarding behaviors are detrimental to hoarders and family members alike, children feel their impact particularly acutely. In this chapter, we explored the emotional, health, safety, quality-of-life, legal, and ethical concerns associated with hoarding, especially when there are children in the house. Hoarding behavior creates a lot of anger, shame, and embarrassment in the family. Besides the negative effects on emotional well-being, hoarding creates health issues due to unsanitary living conditions, insect and other animal infestations, the accumulation of animal waste, and the proliferation of dust and mold. Safety issues include loss of accessibility within the home, factors that increase the risk of and the potential deadliness of a fire, and structural damage. Quality-of-life issues include loss of functional living space, loss of privacy, and loss of opportunities for socializing. Finally, we touched on the legal and ethical implications of hoarding.

In the following chapter, we will more closely examine the emotional impact of hoarding on children who grew up in a home full of clutter, as well as the struggle experienced by adult children who watch helplessly from the periphery. In future chapters, we will suggest strategies aimed at minimizing the impact of the logistical and emotional burden you experience as a result of your parent's hoarding.

CHAPTER 3

Talking to Your Parent about the Problem

WHAT WORKS AND WHAT DOES NOT

Think back to all the different times you felt frustrated, hurt, angry, or in pain because your parent dismissed you, and held on to the possessions instead. At these times, what did you say to your parent? Sometimes you may have said nothing, especially when you were young; at other times you may have tried to say something but been cut short. In the following exercise, we will ask you to examine the ways in which you have tried to influence your parent to change.

Exercise: Examine What You Have Tried

Using a notebook or a separate piece of paper, write down everything you have tried so far to communicate to your parent your unhappiness with his or her hoarding. Write down all the different actions you have taken—both things you have done and things you have said—with regard to your parent's hoarding. Some of these things may not seem like "strategies" because they were spontaneous, not planned; still, that is how we want you to view them for the purposes of this exercise. Here are a few examples provided by children of parents who hoard:

- *I tried quietly telling her that I needed my own space—at least my own bedroom.*

- *I tried crying and telling him that I could not live this way.*

- *I said nothing.*

- *I yelled and screamed and threw a temper tantrum.*

- *I started throwing things away randomly and told her that she had no right to put the family through all this.*

- *I went to live with a friend and told my father that I never wanted to see him again.*

- *I moved out of the house.*

- *I never brought my children over to the house.*

- *I told her that I never wanted her to come to my house because she brings bugs from home.*

- *I told her that I was disgusted by her and the house. They should live in shame forever.*

- *I told him how ashamed I am of where I came from.*

When you have completed your list, for each strategy that you listed, ask yourself, *What did I hope to accomplish in doing or saying that?* Maybe you were hoping to urge your parent to change; maybe you were trying to preserve your own well-being; maybe you were trying to restore a positive relationship with your parent. With the answer to this question in mind, how successful were you in accomplishing what you intended? On a scale of 1 to 5, rate how much better you felt, with 1 indicating no change or negative change; 2 indicating slight improvement; 3 indicating moderate improvement; 4 indicating significant improvement; and 5 indicating drastic improvement. Keep in mind that not every strategy works for everyone, so it's important to determine what will work for you.

Many children of hoarders follow a common path in their relationship with their parent who hoards. They see a problem in their life (their parent's hoarding), and they attempt to understand or tolerate it, negotiate for their space, struggle for some space of their own, or ultimately, try to get their parent to change. The last option is, in most cases, unfeasible, and often leads to more frustration. When years of struggle do not lead to any long-term solutions, trying to get their parent to change becomes too exhausting for these children. Many children of hoarders, after years of no progress and bitter arguing, become estranged from their parent, avoiding all contact and vacillating between guilt, resentment, and worry. Estrangement is not easy at all, and takes years of hard work to heal.

Yelling and making accusations (agitation or aggressive communication), while a natural and logical response to the problems that hoarding creates, is a trap that can lead only to continued fighting or to your giving up and either enabling (accommodating) or distancing yourself from your parent (isolating). So what does work? Or more importantly, what should your goals be in communicating with your parent who hoards? In this chapter, we will attempt to answer those questions. But first, let us go into the specific reasons why what you have tried so far has not had the desired effect. Below, we will explore why both accommodation and agitation are unsuccessful in bringing about change. We will also explore what you might do differently.

ACCOMMODATION

My mom is so dependent on me. I finally moved out three years ago in order to get some distance from the clutter. When I lived at home, my mother relied entirely on me to keep food in the house and to keep the basic necessities under control. I would come home from work to find more and more of her things spilling over into communal spaces or even into areas that were clearly supposed to be mine. All of this made me so angry, but it always just felt like a losing battle. Why bother trying to stop a wave? Sometimes I would try to reclaim my areas, and sometimes I would try to clean up communal areas, but I definitely reached a point where I gave up. The argument that would ensue was not worth it by any stretch. Eventually I moved out, claiming freedom to live the way that I wanted to, but I still get at least two calls from her per day, asking me to

*do one thing or another. She needs groceries on Tuesday; she
needs her medication to be picked up on Wednesday; she
needs me to do her laundry every Thursday because her
machine has been broken for years. Sometimes she calls to
vent about something that my sister said to her. Sometimes she
makes me feel guilty for leaving. I know that her hoarding is
the result of a psychological disorder, but sometimes I just can't
believe how selfish she seems.*

Accommodation in the case of hoarding refers to efforts made by nonhoarders to pacify, live with, or just put up with a dysfunctional lifestyle imposed by the hoarder's behavior. Accommodation equates to enabling the dysfunctional behavior.

Much attention has been paid to the influence of accommodating behaviors among family members of individuals with obsessive-compulsive spectrum behaviors, including hoarding, obsessive-compulsive disorder (OCD), and obsessive-compulsive personality disorder (OCPD). A few examples of accommodation related to obsessive-compulsive behaviors are washing your hands because a compulsive hand washer asks you to, double-checking that doors are closed or locked and that appliances are turned off for someone who has a checking compulsion, not throwing things away in a hoarder's home, not inviting people over to a hoarder's home, ordering out for food all the time because the oven is broken in a hoarder's home, doing laundry outside because the washing machine is inaccessible due to clutter, and sleeping on the couch because the bed is too cluttered (Calvocoressi et al. 1999).

Children of hoarders are often drawn into the compulsive world of their parent who hoards—this means that they may limit their own social experiences if they live with the parent, assume a caregiving role, or keep the grandchildren from visiting the parent's home. Sometimes children of hoarders are asked to or must assume caregiver responsibilities because their parents are unable (e.g., due to physical limitations) or neglect to take care of basic needs (grocery shopping, laundry, etc.). This may be true for you whether or not you live with your parent who hoards. For example, do you have to do laundry for your father because he cannot use his washing machine due to clutter or because it is in disrepair? Have you ever had to bring your mother to your own home on a hot summer day because she did not have a working air conditioner? Have you ever had to care for your father after he was injured when he tripped over something in the clutter? Although you may feel some guilt about accommodating your parent's hoarding lifestyle, *not* accommodating it might mean neglecting your parent's health and safety needs.

You might be surprised to learn that simply keeping quiet about the topic of your parent's hoarding also constitutes accommodation, because it allows the behavior to continue unchecked. Children of hoarders, especially those who live in the house, often fear the anger, tantrums, and even violence that attempts to change the hoarder's behavior or request one's own space can be met with, and they often say nothing. However, walking on eggshells to avoid creating a conflict around your parent's hoarding does nothing to help the situation. And, most importantly, it keeps you from expressing feelings that you are entitled to have and assert.

Accommodation is insidious because it disrupts a healthy family dynamic and makes circumstances that are rightfully unacceptable seem acceptable. When children of hoarders start participating in this dynamic, they are likewise contributing to the unhealthy arrangement. Worse, once family members of hoarders begin accommodating, it is very difficult to break the habit. The bottom line is that you must place limits on your accommodating efforts where health and safety are concerned. Hopefully, by the end of this book, you will feel empowered to take action against the tendency to accommodate, whatever that action will be: whether you choose to have some relationship with your parent outside of his or her hoarding, or to have no relationship at all for the sake of your own well-being. (Regardless of the path you end up taking, try to get some support from friends, siblings, or other family members to help you through it.)

AGITATION

Angela had frequent disagreements with her mother regarding the conditions of her mother's home and the future of her relationship with her mother. She was especially disturbed by the squalor of her mother's home. Her disgust about her mother's living conditions, as well as her frustration with her mother's apparent refusal to change, often spilled out in unproductive ways. One day Angela said, "Mom, that's it. The place is beyond help. Do you not see the cockroaches all over everything? You are just disgusting. I have lived so much of my life feeling completely disgusted. If Dad were alive, he would be so ashamed of what you have let happen to his home. I've truly had it, and I am going to throw it all out."

The above quote illustrates the temptation to *agitate* the situation. Although you can understand how Angela feels and why, expression of these sentiments in this way is not very constructive. As you might expect, Angela's mother did not respond well to Angela's statements. To make matters worse, now, according to her mother, her hoarding is not the problem; Angela is the problem. *Agitation* refers to the expression of negative feelings or behaviors in an explosive manner. Agitation can be both verbal (e.g., aggressive statements) and behavioral (e.g., throwing items away without your parent's consent). Usually the goal is to change the situation for the better, but ultimately agitation serves only to make things worse. Verbal agitation includes criticism, intrusive statements, demands or commands, yelling, or deliberately trying to insult or wound (e.g., Bellack, Haas, and Tierney 1996); behavioral agitation may include efforts to coercively clean up or discard items without a hoarder's consent or awareness. Family members tend to resort to agitation when they feel angry, resentful, frustrated, desperate, or backed into a corner in some other way.

Again, it is very logical and reasonable if you have behaved this way. Unfortunately, this kind of behavior tends to be unconstructive. The bottom line is that acting on impulses born of anger and resentment simply will not work toward affecting any change in your parent's behavior.

However, it must be said that you are completely justified in your frustration, pain, anger, and resentment. Anybody in your situation would be tempted to "fly off the handle" every once in a while. You may have been told that what you feel, think, and report is all in your head. And your freedom was taken away by someone who was supposed to look after your welfare. It does not seem right, and it is not right. The situation you are in is not fair. Given that truth, we are going to ask you to explore not what *would* be right or fair, but rather what will *work* toward achieving the goal of feeling empowered, rather than defeated, in a very difficult situation. Again, your goal may be to establish a better relationship with your parent outside of the hoarding issues, or to stop seeing your parent. However, whatever you choose to save yourself from the myriad of negative emotions, you must at all times remember that hoarding is a manifestation of a psychological problem and not something that your parent has imposed on you willfully, with malicious intent. That the problem infringes on your rights and territory is due to the nature of the disorder.

ISOLATION

Unfortunately, as we mentioned, all too often the end result of vacillating between accommodation and agitation is estrangement. You may feel as though the emotional toll of witnessing the state of your parent's home is too much to handle on a regular basis; if you have children, you may understandably not want to bring them over to your parent's home; or you may find the burden of tending to your parent's health and well-being too daunting to even attempt any longer. Many children of hoarders are in the same boat. If you are considering cutting ties with your parent who hoards, you are not alone by any means, though that may come as little comfort.

The decision to isolate yourself from your parent is a very personal one, and we are not passing judgment on those who make this decision. We believe that you have allegiance and responsibility to yourself first and foremost, and if a relationship with your parent who hoards is truly impossible, then isolation may be the best course of action for you. Certainly you will not be the first person to ever make this decision. Most people who isolate themselves from their parent who hoards do so as a matter of self-preservation, because they feel unable to tolerate the situation in any form anymore, or because they anticipate that the consequences of isolation will be the final, necessary wake-up call that brings about some change in their parent's behavior. Some do so for both of these reasons. *Maybe without my presence or support,* they reason, *my parent will hit rock bottom and realize that something needs to change. And I cannot continue suffering like this anymore.*

However, hoarders can often maintain relatively normal functioning outside the home, so their behavior is not so dysfunctional that their lives become completely unmanageable if they are left to fend for themselves. So while we recognize that isolation may be best for your own emotional health, if your ultimate goal is to change your parent, it likely will not help you do this. Nevertheless, though the decision to isolate yourself from your parent is a very difficult, potentially final decision that will not necessarily have an effect on your parent's perception of the problem, it may be the only solution for your own emotional well-being. It is also a decision that every child of a hoarder will have to make for him- or herself.

Thankfully, there are alternatives to accommodation, agitation, and isolation: namely, assertive communication, understanding, and setting and adhering to boundaries. In the sections that follow, we will explore what each of these strategies may have to offer, and show you how you can use each one.

ASSERTIVE COMMUNICATION

Assertive communication is distinguished from aggressive or passive communication as the most psychologically healthy way of handling confrontation. *Aggressive* communication refers to expression of emotion in a way that violates and blames another person. Some of the example statements in the previous discussion of agitating behaviors would be considered aggressive. Aggressive communication tends to include a lot of "You" statements (e.g., "You are disgusting"; "You're a terrible mother"). And while such statements may feel true, they may not necessarily reflect how you feel overall, nor help the situation. As you may suspect, we are going to advise that you steer clear of this communication style as much as possible.

On the other end of the spectrum (and also unproductive) is *passive* communication, which basically involves swallowing any resentment or displeasure and accepting any abuse that you receive. Passive communication is associated with feelings of defeat and resignation. This communication style is ultimately insidious, as one of two outcomes usually results: either you can no longer hold your tongue and you resort to aggressive communication, or you develop a defeatist mentality, wherein you no longer advocate for yourself or stand up for what you deserve. As you can probably anticipate, this mentality can be very damaging to you in the long term and can lead to feelings of helplessness and loss of motivation.

As we will elucidate, it is important that you strike a balance between the two extremes of aggressive and passive communication. The goal is to communicate your feelings and concerns without dominating the other person or becoming verbally forceful. Walking this fine line involves discussing your feelings honestly and directly, yet without making aggressive statements.

It is important for you to keep the following idea in mind: nothing productive can result when the conversation becomes aggressive. This is important for the person on either end of a dialogue; you will not be able to influence someone once things are said in a spirit of aggression. Assertive communication ensures that your perspective is heard, but also ensures that the other person continues to listen. This is an important skill that, if practiced, will guide you toward more effective communication with your parent who hoards.

In contrast to aggressive communication, assertive communication offers many "I" statements (e.g., "I feel threatened in this house"; "I don't feel as though my feelings about this situation matter to you"; or "I struggle to have the strength to deal with this situation"). Notice the difference in emotional tone between these statements and the aggressive ones above. In both the aggressive and the assertive statements, the same feelings are being communicated: anger, desperation, concern, and worry. However, the assertive statements are much less likely to result in an aggressive response. For this reason, "I" statements are a cornerstone of assertive communication. Other essential elements of assertive communication are acknowledging the other person's perspective and proposing solutions or making suggestions for change.

Following is an example of a conversation in which a daughter whose father started hoarding shortly after her mother died communicates her feelings and concerns assertively, using "I" statements.

> *Stephanie:* Dad, I am really just concerned about how things will proceed from here. You're having health problems, and it's getting harder and harder to maintain safety in this house.

> *Dad:* I don't need you doting on me, Stephanie. I'm fine. I don't know what you mean, as far as my safety… I've lived in this house for forty years, and I don't see why you should think that things are more dangerous for me now.

> *Stephanie:* I feel very frustrated when you tell me that there are no safety issues. I'm concerned when I see how

you maneuver in the house these days! There are very few safe routes from room to room, and I'm just concerned about you falling or something.

Dad: I can see that, Stephanie, but let's not make a · mountain out of a molehill.

Notice in this example how Stephanie's father was willing to engage in a dialogue about his behavior because she did not communicate her perspective on the situation aggressively. She indicated her concerns using "I" statements ("I am really just concerned") and her anger ("I feel very frustrated"), all without acting angry or desperate.

Stephanie's next step was to acknowledge her father's perspective.

Stephanie: I understand that you have lived in this house for forty years—put your soul into it and love it—and do not think that there are any safety issues.

She then made a few suggestions for change:

I was wondering how you would feel if we worked on making your bedroom look more the way it did before Mom died. We could maybe clear off the bed, organize the drawers, and give the room a fresh coat of paint.

In summary, try to do the following three things when communicating about the problem with your parent who hoards:

1. Put your feelings in the form of "I" statements.

2. Acknowledge how your parent feels.

3. Propose a way you can start to tackle the problem together.

UNDERSTANDING HOARDING BEHAVIOR

Though it is difficult to do so, it will be helpful to you to acknowledge the gravity of your parent's feelings about the items being hoarded and about the situation in general in your own process of healing. Even if you cannot fathom why your father, for instance, feels the way that he does, it is important to know that his frame of reference is different than yours and that his feelings about his possessions are very intense. For this reason, it is important to keep in mind that your parent did not choose to live this way. Rather, your parent's unique way of seeing the world contributed to a pattern of behavior that has proven to be detrimental and dangerous. While this pattern of behavior is harmful to everyone who lives in or visits the house, and you have suffered as a result of it, it is also strongly motivated, and understanding these motivations can help you too to come to terms with your own struggle, and move in a productive direction.

Again, if you are honest with yourself, you can probably see that these general statements are true:

- Your parent does feel more intensely about material things than the average person, due to the interaction of unique life circumstances and personal biology.

- You do want your parent to be happy and not dominated by behaviors that do not serve your parent's larger goals in life.

- You need to be validated by your parent for the suffering that hoarding has brought to your own life.

For most of your life, you have not been validated for the feelings you have had as the child of a hoarder. No one has apologized to you for what you had to go through. And you may be thinking to yourself, "How can I be asked to understand this when nobody understands me?" Although it's hard to understand and

59

acknowledge your parent's plight, those who feel they can have a relationship with their parent, outside of hoarding issues, can make statements such as:

- "Mom, I know that you love your fabrics and you want to make quilts out of them."

- "Dad, I know that you spent your career reading and working on computers and want to keep these magazines to read. They mean a lot to you."

- "I know that you are concerned about throwing away these used paper goods because you may accidentally throw away something of value."

Exercise: Craft Your Own Understanding Statements

In a notebook or on a separate piece of paper, list a few points of conflict between you and your parent. List your position on each issue. Now list your parent's position on each issue, and find a statement that demonstrates understanding of this position, as in the example below:

Point of conflict: The cockroach infestation in Mom's house

- *My position: Walking into Mom's house is disgusting due to the infestation, among other examples of squalor. It is undeniable that there is a major health hazard all around her house.*

- *Mom's position: I would love to be able to get rid of the bugs, but too much needs to be done to get to all infested areas. I plan to organize all the items in my house, at which time a proper cleaning will be possible.*

- *Understanding statement: "Mom, I know that the idea of confronting the infestation is really overwhelming. I know that my suggested solutions often involve discarding items in order to get to the problem of the infestation. I now see how threatening this sounds to you, and I just want you to know that I understand that, objectively, you can see that the cockroaches are a problem. I also know that the anxiety you feel about cleaning up makes it very hard for you to take the necessary steps to get rid of the infestation."*

Throughout this section, we've been talking about ways in which you can achieve and express a degree of understanding about your parent's hoarding behavior. At this point, you may well be wishing that your parent would understand how you've suffered as a result of that behavior, and what they're putting you through now. This is also something that needs to happen, and you need to be honest with your parent about your need to be understood, if you intend to have a relationship with him or her.

RULES AND BOUNDARIES

One of the most important things that you can do for yourself is set certain rules and boundaries with your parent who hoards, as far as what you will and will not tolerate, in your own best interest. Children often feel an undying responsibility to make their parents proud of them and to make decisions that their parents will be happy with. This may create an internal struggle for you as the child of a hoarder. You may disagree with many of the things that your parent would have you do, especially if they constitute accommodation. And while some accommodation is inevitable, given the nature of elder care, if that is the case, it is important to establish a dialogue about what you are and are not willing to do in order to ensure your parent's well-being. Again, this is highly personal. You need to be very honest with yourself about what you can do for your parent without sacrificing your own health and well-being.

If you are living with your parent who hoards, setting and adhering to rules and boundaries means having a direct and open dialogue about what areas are "off limits" as places to deposit, keep, or store items being hoarded. This may mean that your parent cannot make use of your personal areas (e.g., your bedroom) or that some degree of usability of communal areas must be respected and maintained (e.g., the kitchen must be restored to enough functionality so that it may be used to prepare meals). These are very reasonable requests, and it is important that you make them in an assertive way.

If you are not living with your parent who hoards, setting and adhering to rules and boundaries relates to what kind of contact you are willing to have with your parent. For example, you should determine how many times per week or per month you are willing to go to your parent's home to help your parent with laundry, cooking, cleaning, or shopping, or how much contact you are willing to have with your parent in general. If you have children, you may also want to establish how frequently or extensively you are willing to have your family interact with your parent who hoards, and under what circumstances you will allow visitation. Many children of hoarders request that their parent visit with the grandchildren only on neutral ground (not at the parent's home), but if you are willing to bring your children into your parent's home, you may want to make it very clear if you have requests or expectations as far as conditions in the home. This may mean asking for things that would seem to go without saying, such as that the toilet and bathroom sink be clean, accessible, and working or that the home be free of any rotting food or insect infestations.

If you and your parent can decide on rules and boundaries together, it will most likely increase the extent to which your parent complies with your requests. However, before entering into these kinds of discussions, be sure to have a framework of what you would like to cover, and be mindful of which issues you will not "bend" on. Be sure to stay firm on these specific issues, and firmly assert your feelings about them. For example, if you are living with your parent, and you are adamant that you deserve adequate private space that is free of your parent's clutter, make this very clear and accept nothing less. Once boundaries are established, it is important that you and your parent do not stray from the plan that you have set in place. This is the time to stand your ground and resist accommodation (not *all* accommodation, but any accommodation that would breach the arrangement that you and your parent have agreed upon).

OPENING A DIALOGUE

With all this in mind—assertive communication, understanding, and rules and boundaries—it is time to open a dialogue with your parent. Rather than a confrontation, consider it a formal discussion: an opportunity to address your feelings, concerns, and requests with your parent in a way that minimizes conflict and promotes a collaborative approach that strengthens your relationship. While you may be presenting your parent with information that may be perceived as threatening (and obviously the conversation will contain some tense moments), this is more of an opportunity to voice yourself in an assertive way and practice the skills discussed above.

After completing the following exercise, you should have a better understanding of what you would like to address (the "framework" we alluded to in the previous section) during your discussion with your parent.

Exercise: Write a Letter to Your Parent

Look back at your responses to the exercise in chapter 2 in which we asked you to consider some of the many ways in which your parent's hoarding may have affected you both as a child and as an adult. The questions were meant to get at how your experiences, feelings, relationships, and thoughts have been influenced by your parent's hoarding.

In your notebook or on a separate sheet of paper, revisit these issues. Compile your responses to the questions we asked in the form of a letter explaining your feelings to your parent who hoards. As you write this letter, try to adhere to some of the strategies described above: practicing assertive communication ("I" statements, acknowledging the other person's perspective, and making suggestions), using under-standing statements, and avoiding agitating or accommodat-ing ones. You will not mail this letter or read it to your parent word for word—this is just an exercise to help you practice effective communication strategies and clarify your thoughts about your history and your parent's hoarding. Hopefully, however, it will serve as a guideline for the discussion that you will soon have with your parent. Following is a sample letter.

Dad, thank you for hearing this: I know how much we have fought about your hoarding in the past, and honestly that is not what I want. I don't mean to argue about this, though I realize that sometimes argument is unavoidable. But there are certain things that I need you to hear about my experiences growing up in this environment. Your hoarding has affected my life in many ways. Specifically, I feel as though I never had the relationships with my friends that I should have had. I was never able to have friends over to the house because it would have been embarrassing for all of us. I felt and still feel very ashamed of many things in my life, which I believe relates back to the shame that I felt about the state of our house. I am not telling you this to blame you; rather, I am trying to tell you very honestly how I have felt throughout the years. I believe that growing up in a home full of clutter affected many of the relationships that I have had. I tend to be secretive and guarded in my relationships for fear of how I will be judged, and it makes me uncomfortable to have other people in my home. I have little tolerance for clutter. When I walk into a cluttered area, I feel so nervous and uncomfortable. Am I saying this to make you feel guilty? No. I want you to hear this—really hear it—and appreciate the impact that hoarding has had on all of our lives, including yours.

The pain that I see you endure as a result of hoarding is immense. You cannot discard anything that you believe has the slightest value; it pains you when you have to part with something that is "yours," and I know that you feel as though your belongings are a part of you. I cannot imagine how that must feel, and I hope never to suffer in that way.

However, I have suffered. It makes me so sad that I do not have much of a relationship with you anymore. I think about this situation constantly, and it tears me apart. I miss my dad; my kids miss their grandfather. I really just want to have a different relationship with you. I want to find a way to have a less argumentative dialogue about all the stuff you keep. I am willing to do my part and try to communicate with you differently, with more sensitivity for your feelings about this. I am asking you to do the same with me, as well.

Having clarified your thoughts in this way, and having rehearsed in writing what you want to say in a manner both assertive and understanding, choose a time and a place to meet with your parent who hoards. When you get together with your parent, do not bring the letter with you, but try to remember the things you wrote about and insert them as naturally as possible in the conversation. The goal is to open up a healthier dialogue with your parent about the

problem. We cannot stress enough the importance of staying assertive and keeping your pain from thwarting your efforts at communication. In the following chapters, we will elaborate on how to
foster a better relationship with your parent while maintaining the
boundaries that you have set in place.

SUMMARY

The aim of this chapter was to help you see how your own actions
and the way in which you communicate or do not communicate
about your parent's hoarding might not do much to solve the
problem. Specifically, you may be accommodating your parent, agitating the situation, or doing both these things at different times.
In this chapter, we asked you to bring awareness to your responses
to your parent, which in the past may have been either too aggressive or too passive. We explained some principles of assertive communication and understanding, and you practiced using them,
laying the groundwork for a discussion with your parent about your
feelings and concerns so that you can have a constructive conversation that includes setting rules and boundaries. In future chapters, we will elaborate on techniques aimed at improving your
relationship with your parent or preserving your own emotional
well-being.

CHAPTER 4

Managing Your Reactions and Coping with Your Emotions

A MINDFULNESS- AND ACCEPTANCE-ORIENTED APPROACH

I n this chapter, we will explore mindfulness- and acceptance-oriented strategies for managing your unpleasant emotional reactions to your parent's hoarding.

It may stir up some of that resentment that we discussed in previous chapters to consider what we are asking you to consider as goals in this chapter. It is totally understandable if you feel as though you should not have to be the one to change, and that you should not have to *cope* with your emotions; rather, you should not have to have them in the first place, because you should not even be in this situation! And as true as that is, it still leaves you in the same predicament and feeling the same way.

The approach that we are proposing is about trying to do what will work, rather than operating on principle. Yes, you are right that it is not fair if you live in a home full of clutter thanks to your parent who hoards; no one should have to put up with that. Yet, your parent has not changed in regard to the problem and probably will not change in the near future, and the only person you have control over is yourself. So, the best thing you can do right now is work on letting go of your emotional baggage and moving in the direction of what is important to you in life.

ACCEPTANCE VS. CHANGE

When faced with a problem or a dilemma, you have two choices: accept it or try to fix it (change the situation). Some problems are inherently impossible to fix (e.g., the effects of a chronic disabling condition), while some are easily fixed (e.g., being out of toilet paper). Subjects of psychological discomfort (e.g., both your parent's hoarding and your emotional reaction to it) generally lie somewhere in between. So while there are practical things that you can do to minimize the clutter, the way that the clutter affects you, your parent's functioning, and the problem as a whole represents a chronic and unchanging aspect of your life.

In other words, some things in life will change, some will not change, and some may eventually change. Based on this, it is easy to see why acceptance may be an important coping mechanism for anyone to adopt: for dealing with both the things in life that will not change and the uncertainty that comes with waiting for other things to change. It is important for us to point out that when we talk about accepting discomfort, such as feeling upset because your parent is not changing, it is not the same as accepting that your parent will never change. Acceptance of discomfort can work hand in hand with efforts to improve the situation.

The human brain is a problem-solving machine. As such, it is constantly seeking out problems and coming up with solutions. For example, if your mother hoards magazines, you might think: *There are piles of magazines all over the living room. Maybe Mom should get a professional organizer to help her arrange her magazines in an orderly fashion. I can find professional organizers on the Internet!* Problem and solution. The problem-solving brain is successful in correcting many problems. However, it frequently hits dead ends with regard to the problem of hoarding. This is because hoarders are very resistant to change. Thus you may sit down with your mother countless times and give her all the reasons that you can think of for her to change the way she is living, only for her to call you a meddler and accuse you of interfering with her business. It may seem that nothing gets through.

Acceptance relates to the idea of yielding to your day-to-day experience and allowing it to happen without attempting to change or manipulate it—allowing it to be exactly what it is. When you accept what is going on and accept what you feel, you will feel more at peace and have a higher sense of well-being. This is not to say that we recommend neglecting opportunities for change. On the contrary, if you can complete certain concrete activities—for example, if your parent is willing to discard items and you can help—then by all means go for it if you would like to. Obviously, change can be beneficial. But emotional acceptance of both things that can and things that cannot be changed allows you to accept the reality of your situation, peacefully. When you are living without clinging to your expectations about how things should be, you will find that you remain steady during periods of uncertainty. This is especially useful when dealing with circumstances that have remained unchanging for many frustrating years.

ACCEPTANCE AND COMMITMENT THERAPY (ACT)

Acceptance and commitment therapy (ACT; Hayes, Strosahl, and Wilson 1999) explores the idea of acceptance in the face of both everyday and not-so-everyday frustration, while you live your life according to your values. We will go into greater depth about the specifics of this challenge further on in this chapter, but it will suffice to say for the time being that we propose a strategy for "letting go" of your struggle against your feelings and abandoning the pursuit of *emotional* control or improvement. Instead, we propose trying to live a better life despite the circumstances of your parent's ongoing hoarding. There are six central ideas in ACT: acceptance/willingness, mindfulness, cognitive defusion, values clarification, committed action, and self-as-context.

Acceptance/Willingness

According to the theory underlying ACT (Hayes, Strosahl, and Wilson 1999), unpleasant emotions—such as anger, anxiety, disgust, fear, or resentment—are not "bad," nor are they necessarily evidence of a psychological problem. They are an unavoidable aspect of human existence. And psychological dysfunction is caused not by unpleasant emotional experiences, but rather by people's responses to them. For example, if your mother feels anxious at the thought of passing up an opportunity to buy clearance clothing items from a department store, she can either (a) give in to the urge to buy the items, thereby reducing her anxiety, or (b) *sit with* (that is, make no effort to reduce or avoid) that anxiety until it goes away. If she consistently chose to sit with her anxiety, then her home would be less cluttered or possibly not cluttered at all. Or if your mother threw more things away even though it made her uncomfortable or upset, then again there would not be so much clutter. In both instances, it is not the urge to acquire or the aversion to throwing things out but the inability to sit with discomfort that leads to hoarding. The problem lies in the way your mother (in this example) handles her discomfort, rather than the discomfort itself. This point is important, because the challenge for both you and your parent who hoards is to accept the presence of anxiety, discomfort, or disgust without trying to adjust, manipulate, or banish it. For your parent, this would mean accepting the urge to acquire (which is a state of discomfort) and letting that urge exist without acting on it. For you, this means accepting what you see when you walk into your parent's house, as well as your reactions to it (e.g., anger, fear, disgust, or resentment), and allowing those feelings to be there without becoming hostile toward your parent, throwing things away without your parent's consent, and so forth.

In the context of ACT, in other words, acceptance means sitting with unpleasant feelings (especially when little can be done to fix the situation) while deliberately pursuing what is important to you in life. Assuming that a good relationship with your parent is important to you, this may mean accepting your resentment about your parent's hoarding while communicating your feelings in a productive way. On the other hand, practicing acceptance does not mean that you must always do things that make you uncomfortable, if you have a choice. For example, if you value spending time with your parent, but the state of your parent's house bothers you, you can find ways to spend time with your parent outside of the house. However, sometimes in life your options will be limited— there will be no way to act in accordance with your values and do what is important to you without suffering some discomfort—and in these cases acceptance is the best way forward.

Acceptance, as we hinted above, does not mean resigning yourself to the fact that things will never get better. Acceptance is, purely and simply, willingness to experience what is in front of you or inside of you. Acceptance does not require you to feel differently about your parent's hoarding or to change your mind at all about any situation. It is less of an attitude change and more of a behavioral change. It is about being willing to behave in ways that might put you in contact with unpleasant feelings and staying present to (or not "shutting down" to) your emotional experiences as they arise.

The benefit of willingness is far reaching. If you are willing to have a feeling, you can always make the most out of the present moment. Most dysfunction in life arises as a result of refusal to have unwanted feelings and failure to act according to what is meaningful. Let us say that a college student with depression finds it emotionally painful to get out of bed and refuses to have this pain. Thus, the only thing he can do is stay in bed. He does not particularly value staying in bed or find it meaningful—he values furthering his education by attending classes and earning a degree—but it is easier than dragging himself to classes. His staying in bed, however, results in his neglect of those things that he does value and find meaningful; he misses important opportunities for learning and does not move closer to his goal of earning a degree. If he were willing to have the unpleasant feelings that came with getting out of bed, depression might not stop him from doing what was important to him in life.

The following exercise is intended to allow you to practice a stance of willingness with regard to your feelings about your parent's hoarding.

Willingness Exercise

In a notebook or on a separate piece of paper, write down some things you have avoided because of your parent's hoarding. For example:

- *Talking to my parent on the phone*

- *Going into my parent's house*

- *Inviting my parent to my house to visit with my children*

We get that it is often easier to avoid the unpleasant feelings—of resentment, anger, or anxiety—that doing these things may cause. Right now, however, we want you to practice doing the opposite: inviting your unpleasant feelings and sitting with them. As ACT therapists frequently say, willingness is like jumping. While there are big jumps and there are small jumps, jumping is an all-or-nothing proposition (Hayes, Strosahl, and Wilson 1999, 241). In order to be successful, you must do it decisively. You must be open to your experience and any discomfort you might feel. So take a couple of slow, deep breaths, then follow these steps:

1. Pick one thing you wrote that you have avoided. Try to pick something that avoidance of which gets in the way of what you would like to do (e.g., have a pleasant conversation with your parent, see your parent more often, or have your children get to know their grandparent), and focus on a specific thought or image related to what you have avoided that evokes an unpleasant feeling.

2. Close your eyes, and imagine doing the very thing you have avoided.

3. As the scene unfolds in your imagination, will yourself to stay present to your discomfort. Imagine what you

73

would hope to accomplish by doing so in real life. What would be important for you to do in spite of your feelings? Try to visualize yourself doing it.

4. Each time that your mind tries to pull you away from imagining doing what you have avoided, direct your mind back to the task and really try to welcome the emotion with a sense of willingness. Continue doing this for about ten minutes.

Afterward, note how your mind tried to divert you from the task. Notice how sitting with these thoughts and feelings with willingness is a departure from what your mind would typically urge you to do. Notice how present-moment focus, as well as attention to your thoughts and feelings, results in a different outcome. The feelings may still be intense, but notice how you are able to sit with them through willingness to have them.

As you develop mindfulness (explored below), awareness of internal and external cues will allow you to better notice when you are avoiding certain thoughts and feelings and how to let your values (also explored below) guide you through these situations. For example, if you are presented with the task of calling your parent to set up a time and a place to meet, you might have the urge to avoid this task. Mindfulness skills will allow you to recognize this urge, and with consideration for your values, you may choose a more deliberate, value-oriented approach, such as choosing a meeting place and a time that you can tolerate.

Mindfulness

Mindfulness refers to present-moment focus and attention to your immediate experiences, both internal and external. Mindfulness is about observation, not evaluation; about allowing your experiences and emotions to ebb and flow, rather than striving to cling to positive experiences and eliminate negative ones. Because mindfulness is all about observing, practice of mindfulness involves constantly redirecting yourself to observe things around you without judging them. Mindfulness exercises, or meditations, are intended to foster the skill of "bringing yourself back" to what is immediately in front of you.

Mindfulness may be especially useful to children of hoarders as a means of managing the distress of witnessing hoarding behavior or living with a parent who hoards. However, mindfulness can also help anyone focus on the present moment to reduce worries about the future or break free of rumination over past events.

Below is an example of a *sitting meditation*. In this exercise, you merely notice the sensations associated with one of the simpler human experiences: sitting and breathing. While you may normally take notice of your breathing only rarely—for example, when you are short of breath or breathing anxiously—this vital process is one of the most constant things in your life, and you are always able to tap into the sensation of breathing to ground yourself in the present moment. Do not criticize or judge the exercise—just do it.

Sitting Meditation

Find a quiet place where you will not be disturbed. Assume a comfortable position, and close your eyes. Let go of any thoughts or worries that might presently come to your awareness, and bring your attention to your breathing. Notice the sensation of air traveling into your nose or mouth as you breathe in. Notice the coolness of the air as it passes through these areas. Now feel the air traveling deep into your lungs and abdomen. Notice the relief that you feel as a deep breath provides your body with necessary, life-sustaining oxygen. As you breathe out, notice the relief you feel as your body expels carbon dioxide. Notice how the air that you breathe out is warmer than the air that you breathed in. Maintain your attention on the sensations of this experience. If you notice that your mind has wandered away from this task, just gently redirect your awareness back to your breathing. Some people find it helpful to count their breaths from one to ten, and then repeat, as a means of staying present to the activity. Keep this up for a few minutes.

Afterward, notice the difference in your feelings as you go on with your day. Do you feel more present for your experiences? Are you more focused on what you are doing?

Try practicing sitting meditation for five minutes three times a day. This will help you relax and not obsess about your parent's hoarding. It will allow you to bring awareness to the "here and now." Mindfulness will be especially useful in approaching the task of cognitive defusion, which is explored below.

Cognitive Defusion

As we mentioned, the human brain is a problem-identifying and problem-solving organ, plain and simple. In the same way that you cannot tell your heart to stop beating, you cannot tell your brain to stop looking for and trying to solve problems. For this reason, your brain is rarely focused on the present, especially if there is no immediate problem to be solved. Instead, it likes to take you on a convoluted journey through past struggles, as well as the potential for future dangers. This tends to be a meandering and sometimes frantic process. Furthermore, as the brain is very good at making memories and other images seem real and immediate, you may feel all the emotional turmoil that was present at the time of past distressing events, as well as feel fear of distress in the future. The tendency for us humans to believe that all our thoughts, feelings, and other internal experiences accurately reflect reality is referred to as *cognitive fusion*. Basically, this means that you are predisposed to "buy into" what your mind tells you. You tend not to sit with an objective, unbiased impression of your thoughts; rather, you believe wholesale what your mind says that you should believe.

To illustrate this point, take three minutes to let your mind wander. Close your eyes and let go of the reins. At first you may find this hard to do, as the mere mention of observing your thinking causes increased focus. But as we have mentioned, the observing standpoint is not easy to maintain, so no doubt you will soon be off on a journey with your mind. At the end of three minutes, look back on what you thought about. Try to trace your thought process back to the beginning. If you are like most people who try this exercise, your thought process followed some logical progression: one thought led to another, and that one led to another. What theme did your mind focus on? Was it insisting on attention to your grocery list? Was it drawing you into a depressing spiral of negative thoughts about your parent's hoarding or other distressing aspects of your life? With all that effort that your mind put into whatever it pursued in those three minutes, how many important problems were solved? Likely, very few, especially if your thoughts centered on your parent's hoarding. Even though your parent's hoarding is a chronic problem and not one you can fix, it may seem urgent to your problem-solving brain.

We are certainly not proposing that a *lack of* thinking would be superior to the problem-oriented hyperfocus that the brain tends to employ. On the contrary, the reason why the brain has developed this tendency is because it is the central process that uncovers solutions to life's problems. However, it is not a very efficient process— the brain uses a lot of energy going around and around; most of its time is spent in thinking about problems but not actually solving them.

To illustrate this point, imagine a gold-sluicing machine that sorts gold nuggets from dirt. Let us say that the machine can go through 1,000 bags of dirt per day. Let us say that only one out of every 1,000 bags contains any gold. Well, the machine still has to go through the other 999 bags in order to get to the one that contains the jackpot. Your brain operates the same way; the only way that you are going to isolate that solution to your parent's hoarding is if you pore over every possible thought on the subject. Now let us imagine that the sluicing machine has sorted all 1,000 bags and has found no gold. What does the machine do now? Sorting through dirt is the only thing that it *can* do, and the same enormous quantity of dirt is still in the vicinity. The gold has to be there somewhere, right? So the machine starts sluicing the same dirt again. When it comes to the mind's response to a problem, this pattern can repeat over and over again, as the brain cannot possibly sit restfully, and it only has the same few ever-nagging issues at its disposal. The brain anxiously awaits that shred of confirmation that it has discovered a plan to solve this problem. And even if you were able to solve the problem of your parent's hoarding, we almost guarantee that your brain would find some new problem to focus on!

So if you cannot stop the brain from "sluicing," in our example, or ruminating, and problems are sometimes unchanging and unmanageable, a vicious cycle becomes obvious. So how can you possibly intervene? *Cognitive defusion* is one way to break this cycle. Cognitive defusion involves allowing for some emotional distance from your thinking, or "getting a little cognitive breathing room."

Bring to mind a chilling movie or television show that you have seen. Try to remember the feelings that you experienced while watching the images on the screen. You likely felt an emotional reaction, but it was muted or dulled because of the distance, both environmental and psychological, from the material depicted. The emotional reaction that you felt was not "real" in the same way that your thoughts and feelings typically feel real. Our aim is to develop a way of approaching your own thoughts with the same clarity and distance as if you were watching your life as a movie.

When practicing cognitive defusion, your aim will be to sit resolutely and observantly with unpleasant feelings, without trying to distract yourself from them. You might find that this is a tall order. Not only is it difficult to keep your mind focused on what you are currently experiencing, it can be emotionally painful.

Following is a classic ACT exercise intended to help you achieve "cognitive breathing room," allowing the mind to focus on whatever it will while you focus on the experience of thinking, rather than getting caught up in the specific content of thoughts (Hayes, Strosahl, and Wilson 1999). This exercise involves immediately observing each thought as it occurs, one after another. The purpose is to notice whenever there is a shift from looking *at* your thoughts to looking *from* your thoughts. You will be aware that this has happened when you get caught up in the "current" of your mind. Thought observation is a relatively simple concept, but it is nearly impossible to keep it up for more than a short time, as you may observe when practicing the following meditation.

"Leaves in a Stream" Meditation

Find a quiet place where you will not be disturbed for approximately fifteen to twenty minutes, and assume a comfortable position, either seated, or lying down. Close your eyes and focus on your breathing for a moment. Now imagine yourself standing over a stream, looking down at the water as the current carries it from one side of your field of vision to the other. Just try to hold on to this image for a minute, and get a feel for the speed and rhythm of the flow. The water in this meditation represents the flow of information through your consciousness. Your mind is a constantly moving stream of consciousness, and this flow of information typically occurs completely below the level of your attention. This exercise is intended to bring your awareness to this process as it unfolds.

Now imagine that floating in the current are leaves that are being carried downstream one at a time. One by one, the leaves enter and leave your field of vision. Now imagine that each thought that occurs to you is being projected onto a leaf as it passes. As a thought comes to you, let it fall into the stream and float away with the current. When a thought passes from one side of your field of vision to the other, let go of that thought and make room for the next one.

Your task is to just watch the flow of leaves, without making it stop and without jumping down into the water and chasing a thought downstream. Just let the current flow. It is very unlikely, however, that you can do this without interruption, which is the key part of this exercise. At some point, you will have the sense that the stream has stopped or disappeared, that you have lost the point of the exercise, or that you have floated downstream with a thought instead of just observing it from the bank of the stream. When that happens, back up a few seconds to see whether you can catch what you were thinking or feeling right before you got carried away. Thoughts that tend to carry you off may fall into the category of "sticky" thoughts (troubling, obsessive, and/or attention-demanding thoughts). Children of hoarders often describe thoughts about their parents and the hoarding situation as "sticky" on account of the fact that these thoughts tend to cause a great deal of distress and urgently demand solutions. Notice whether you can trace your deviation from the task of watching the flow of leaves back to a sticky thought. Then go ahead and imagine your thoughts on leaves again until the stream disappears a second time, and continue this cycle. Your main objective is to notice when the flow stops for any reason and to see whether you can catch what happened right before it stopped. Notice how the thoughts that pull you away from observing the flow are often thoughts associated with problem solving, rumination, and/or obsession about things that are troubling.

The purpose of this exercise is not to keep your mind from "wandering off" nor to change the content of your thoughts, but merely to notice the behavior of your mind: what it thinks about and what carries it away. With practice, you may be able to foster more of an "observer" orientation with regard to the content of your thoughts, paving the way for behavioral (as opposed to emotional) control. Bringing awareness to the pull of avoidance of your thoughts and feelings may facilitate deliberate action, providing you with important leverage over your psychological struggles.

Values Clarification

ACT emphasizes the need to live according to your values. ACT therapists often ask their clients, "What would you like your life to stand for?" Or in other words, what are the issues that stand most central to who you are as a person? Values-clarification exercises, such as the one below, adapted from the work of Steven Hayes and Spencer Smith (2005), are intended to bring valued life areas to the forefront, in order to act as a compass for your future. If your values are determining your behavior, you are likely to go in the best direction possible for you, based on what is important to you.

Values-Clarification Exercise

This exercise is intended to determine (1) your valued life areas and (2) how successfully you have been living by your values. Ultimately, this exercise will help you direct your attention to life areas that need more of your focus and time. Anyone can find the following exercise useful, because we all can improve our lives by self-reflection and committed action (explored later in this chapter).

In the following chart are ten life areas that people commonly value, though not everyone values all these areas the same. In the "Importance" column, rate how important each area is to you on a scale of 0 to 10, and in the "Success" column, rate how successfully you have pursued each area in your life so far on a scale of 0 to 10. If any other life areas are important to you, add them and rate them too.

Your parent's hoarding likely siphons a lot of your logistical and psychological resources. And in our experience, children of hoarders tend to neglect other things that are important to them as a sacrifice to their parent's hoarding (i.e., accommodation, as we described it in the previous chapter). This is done with the best of intentions, and anyone in your situation would feel as though your parent's hoarding was the life area requiring the most urgent intervention, but it is important to deliberately prioritize other valued areas, despite your mind's protest. This chart will allow you to identify areas that are important to you but are being neglected. Review your ratings, looking for discrepancies. If you rated the importance of an area a 10 and your success in that area a 2, for example, this is an area to focus on.

Value	Importance 0–10	Success 0–10
Parenting		
Marriage/Couple/Intimate Relationship		
Other Family Relations		
Friendship/Social Relations		
Career/Employment		
Education/Training/Personal Growth		
Citizenship		
Recreation/Leisure		
Spirituality		
Health/Physical Well-Being		
Other:		
Other:		

Whether or not you feel successful in your relationship with your parent, you likely recognize based on this exercise how your parent's hoarding (or perhaps your accommodation of your parent's hoarding) has interfered with your pursuit of other things in life that you value. In the following section, we will explore ways of bringing balance to your life by pursuing other areas.

Committed Action

If you know what is important to you, what stops you from pursuing it? Maybe the problem of your parent's hoarding seems so dire that nothing else feels as important. Maybe you feel unable to set boundaries with your parent, so you put your own happiness and health aside for your parent. Maybe you feel as if you do not have the money, time, or energy. Or maybe you feel so troubled by your past experiences growing up in a home full of clutter that you cannot move forward in the present moment. *Committed action* is all about putting these restrictions aside and pursuing your values, despite all the reasons that your mind provides as to why this is impossible. Pursuing your values is not impossible by any means, although it is not easy. It stands to reason: if it were easy, you would have simply followed your values and attained a well-balanced life long ago; you would not have picked up this book as a means of coping with your inevitably uncomfortable situation.

Clarifying your values and practicing acceptance will allow you to pursue committed action. In other words, committed action involves knowing what you want and being willing to endure the discomfort that accompanies the pursuit of it. Failure to act according to your values often boils down to avoidance of discomfort. Consider a difficult situation that you have faced with regard to your parent's hoarding. How did you handle it, or how are you handling it? What motivated your choices? Were your behaviors planned in line with your values, or were they rather meant to avoid some kind of discomfort? Sometimes it is hard to know what action best suits your values in a certain situation. However, if you know what you need to do at this juncture in your life, but are holding back from doing it because it would cause you too much discomfort, this behavior might be a good target for an exercise in committed action.

Exercise in Committed Action

Jennifer found that she would sometimes avoid calling her father because of the frustration and resentment that she typically felt following their phone conversations. She was also unwilling to go to his house due to the negative feelings that the clutter provoked. She preferred to meet her father in a neutral location (a coffee shop) for conversations. Despite the fact that she was technically willing to meet up with her father, she was extremely reluctant to do so and would often screen his phone calls for months at a time. Even seeing her father triggered unpleasant feelings, and, while in his presence, she would go through elaborate efforts to distance herself from him or distract herself from her feelings about the clutter.

Jennifer's exercise in committed action was to be willing to truly feel whatever feelings came up during a deliberate challenge of her choosing (meeting her father for coffee), without trying to distract or distance herself from them. Clearly this would require a lot of mindfulness (awareness of her emotional reaction to being in her father's presence), as well as acceptance of the discomfort that would arise. The exercise was not a purposelessly painful one, as her relationship with her father was important to her. The activity had meaning to her, and that is why it represents committed action.

Choose some area of your life that you, like Jennifer, have neglected due to avoidance of discomfort. In a notebook or on a separate piece of paper, write down an action that you refrain from that you believe is in line with a neglected value in your life. For Jennifer, it was spending more time with her parent, whereas for you, it might be setting boundaries with your parent that will allow you more independence. The action that you choose is highly individual. It does not have to be the most difficult action you can think of; as long as to carry it out would be in the spirit of committed action (values plus acceptance), rather than avoidance, you are on the right track. Then answer the following questions in order to prepare for committed action:

- *What motivates your avoidance of this behavior?*

- *If your values were determining your behavior, what would you do differently?*

- *What would you be willing to do, according to your values, in the near future?*

- *When would be a good opportunity to do this?*

Self-As-Context

Exercise: Identify Your Self-Labels

In a notebook or on a separate piece of paper, complete the following phrase: "I am…" Come up with as many responses as you can. Some of your responses may be descriptive: for example, "I am a mother"; "I am an accountant"; or "I am a husband." Some of your responses may be judgments: for example, "I am incompetent"; "I am unattractive"; or "I am overwhelmed."

Notice how all these statements vary in their degree of truth. And while they all may represent aspects of how you behave in life, we ask you to consider, are they all *true*? Are some of them painful and nagging (e.g., "I am incompetent at fixing my dad's hoarding behavior")? Notice that, while these labels vary according to their objective accuracy, your mind tries to get you to buy into them as gospel, no matter how subjective they are. If this sounds to you like cognitive fusion, then you are getting the theme, as far as your mind's behavior.

Your mind is invested in getting you to subscribe to your self-labels, and it expects you to act according to them. Thoughts about who you are are some of the hardest to cognitively defuse. It is hard not to buy into the labels you put on yourself. The question is are these labels and how you act as a result of owning them helping you function any better?

ACT seeks to bring awareness to such labels and identify how they may hinder you from moving forward in your life. For example, the label "child of a hoarder" can be particularly loaded. Based on how you approach this self-identification, you may feel compelled to be completely enmeshed in your parent's hoarding, or you may want to be completely removed from it. Neither of these responses is usually in line with committed action.

Instead of behavior according to labels, ACT proposes acknowledgment of the "observer self," which is neither a label nor a role that you fulfill in life. Rather, it is an aspect of you that has been with you throughout your life, witnessing your experiences and your choices. It is not specifically composed of your feelings, your expectations, your thoughts, your physical body, or even the content of your experiences; it is a transcendent part of you that has always observed all these things. The "observer self" is often referred to as "self-as-context" (in contrast with "self-as-content"). Getting in touch with your observer self helps you realize that you are not your thoughts (the content of your mind) but the context in which these thoughts occur. The following exercise, adapted from Steven Hayes, Kirk Strosahl, and Kelly Wilson (1999, 193–95), will elucidate this concept.

"Observer Self" Meditation

Find a quiet place where you will not be disturbed, and settle into a comfortable position. Bring your attention to your surroundings. Look around you; what do you observe? Just take notice of what is around you and realize that there is a distinction between what you are looking at and the "you" who is looking. Just pay attention for a minute to the experience of observing, trying to get a sense of the line that exists between "you" and the world you see.

Now turn your attention to whatever your body is touching. If you are holding this book, pay attention to the way it feels in your hands. Pay attention to the feeling of the furniture, floor, or ground supporting you. Just focus for a minute on the physical sensations of being in contact with these objects, noticing the distinction between these objects and the "you" who senses them.

Now notice your body. Your body is yours, but it is not "you." You can look at, feel, and receive messages from the parts of your body; however, "you" are the one observing your body. For a minute, just concentrate on what it feels like to be aware of your body and anything your body is informing you of by way of internal sensations, noticing the distinction between the body that you feel and see and the "you" who is feeling and seeing.

Now turn your attention to your feelings and thoughts. You are greatly invested in your feelings and thoughts; they may have given you a lot of grief as you tried to manage your experiences as a child of a hoarder. Just like messages from your body, your thoughts and feelings inform you of things that may be important for you to know. Notice that, like your body, your thoughts and feelings are not "you." Notice that you can observe your thoughts and feelings, and notice the "you" who is noticing. Again, notice the distinction between the thoughts and feelings that you observe and the "you" who observes them.

Turn your attention to your firmly held ideas about who you are, what traits you possess, what roles you fulfill, what type of person you are, and so on. Think about how you typically describe yourself. You may be very invested in these self-concepts. Notice that you can feel like an "honest" person, an "isolated" person, or a "worthless" person. Notice how you may be more or less invested in these labels at different moments, depending on what you are doing. For example, sometimes you are a "student," sometimes you are a "daughter," and sometimes you are an "employee." Notice how each of these roles is situation specific; the only constant here is something in you that underlies the transience of thoughts, feelings, roles, self-concepts, and scenery. See whether you can notice the distinction between what you believe about yourself and the "you" who believes.

Finally, notice the "you" that is the point from which all these observations are made. This, your point of reference, is the only place that can truly be called "here" or "now," and it is the only thing that has remained constant throughout your whole life. Whether quickly or slowly, the objects in your environment, your body, your thoughts and feelings, and even your roles and your strongly held beliefs about yourself have changed over your lifetime. The only thing that stays with you through all of it is the "here" or "you" that is observing these changes. Therefore, rather than the *content* of your experiences (your environment, thoughts and feelings, sensations, beliefs, etc.), maybe it is more accurate to imagine your self as the *context* of your life, the setting for all your experiences.

Notice that all the thoughts and feelings that you have been struggling with and trying to change are not "you." See whether you can let go of your self-labels a bit, aware in the knowledge that you have been "you" through everything that you have been through. All of the psychological content—the highs and lows, the pleasant and unpleasant experiences—were never "you" to begin with, so you need not become so entangled and invested in them.

SUMMARY

In this chapter, we explored concepts and techniques of acceptance and commitment therapy (ACT). The aim of ACT is to help people live a more balanced life according to what is important to them, and we believe that the techniques explored in this chapter are useful to children of hoarders. The six facets of this approach are:

- *Acceptance/willingness*: an orientation of willingness to experience thoughts, feelings, and events, whether pleasant or unpleasant, without trying to change them or escape their emotional consequences

- *Mindfulness*: present-moment focus; attention to what you are currently experiencing

- *Cognitive defusion*: seeing thoughts as "just thoughts," rather than buying into them wholeheartedly

- *Values clarification*: identification of those areas in life that are of the utmost importance to you (what you would like your life to "stand for")

- *Committed action*: behavioral commitment to pursue valued life areas, rather than escape from or avoid discomfort

- *Self-as-context*: decreasing your identification with the labels that you place on yourself and learning how to behave in a flexible way

We explored these ideas using exercises and examples to help you practice acceptance as a means of moving forward in areas of life that you value.

If you are interested, there are many acceptance and mindfulness resources out there to expand your understanding and application of the concepts explored in this chapter. For example, while it is not written specifically for children of hoarders, you may find the book by Steven Hayes and Spencer Smith titled *Get Out of Your Mind and Into Your Life* (New Harbinger Publications, 2005) to be useful.

CHAPTER 5

Tools for Coping Specifically with Anger, Depression, and Disgust

As we explored in chapter 2, you are likely to feel a host of emotions as the child of a hoarder. The goal of this chapter is to provide you with a variety of strategies for overcoming the obstacles that your negative emotions may place in your path. These strategies come predominantly from cognitive behavioral therapy (CBT, explained below), and all are aimed at minimizing the influence that unpleasant emotions have over your behaviors.

It is important to mention that the goal here is not necessarily to remove or dull your unpleasant feelings. As we introduced in chapter 4, which explored acceptance-oriented strategies, fighting against your feelings and trying to just "feel better" tends to do more harm than good. Rather, we propose a behavioral system of acknowledging emotional experiences and impulses, with attention to what provokes them, as well as what is best for you and suits your values in the long term. We will also propose cognitive behavioral techniques, such as exposure to unpleasant feelings, which will allow you to confront your unpleasant emotional experiences so as to make emotionally difficult, but important choices.

Perhaps the best way to begin to heal from guilt, shame, anger, depression, or disgust is through forgiveness, so let us begin with that subject.

FORGIVENESS

Take your time when figuring out what "forgiveness" is really about. We are not speaking of forgiveness in the sense in which the word is often used; it is not a dismissal of your pain or frustration, or an exoneration of another for decisions and behaviors for which he or she should be held responsible. Rather, we define forgiveness as a way to demonstrate that you accept events, your feelings about events, and the reality that people are who they are—that your parent is a hoarder, and you are the child of a hoarder—despite your desire for things to be different. And forgiveness, in this sense, becomes a way for you to prepare to make peace with the situation as it is, in order to make decisions in your life based on what is best for you, and what suits your values.

Forgiving your parent who hoards may initially seem like an impossible feat given what you have been through. Even if you have not had to suffer living in your parent's clutter, you may be estranged from your parent after many vicious arguments, or you may have sacrificed too much for your parent to ever restore balance to the relationship. You may feel, on principle, as though your parent does not deserve your forgiveness for the neglect you have experienced. But let us say this: forgiveness is not something that you do for the other person (in this case, your parent); it is something that you do for yourself. Harboring hatred, anger, and resentment toward your parent serves only to hinder your acceptance of the situation and your ability to make peace with the struggles of your past. It may be especially hard to forgive your parent's hoarding behavior if your parent shows no remorse for how it has affected you. But again, you are not doing this for your parent; you are doing this for yourself so that you may move forward in your own life.

If you are not ready for this step, take heart that we understand why it would be difficult for you. Anyone in your situation would struggle to forgive the events of your upbringing and all that has transpired since. Perhaps you will find it easier to forgive your parent if you consider that contradiction in personal values is a hallmark of hoarding behavior. Hoarders want to be responsible; they want to value the people in their lives; they want to prevent deprivation; but they have a misguided way of pursuing these values. For this reason, it is important that loved ones find it in themselves to forgive hoarders for their actions over the years, with the understanding that these actions were rooted in a place of anxiety, dread, and sentimental yearning to hang on to all things that represent their lives and the lives of their loved ones. It may be that, though you can understand your parent's behavior by this point, it is still too much to forgive them, even in this sense; you may need to detach yourself and let go instead. Keep in mind that you need to act in accordance with your feelings and values, and that it's okay to take some time when moving through this process. However, be mindful too of the fact that, for many hoarders, so many items seem like important memorabilia that they are desperate to save them all, and little seems more important than maximizing the potential use of items, both for sentimental acknowledgment and for utilitarian practical applications.

Exercise: Write a Forgiveness Letter

Here, we ask that you compose a letter, which you do not necessarily have to share with your parent. In this letter, you will outline the ways in which you understand that your parent's impulses are difficult for him or her to live with, that you believe that your parent was not looking to inflict pain upon the family, and yet that circumstances that seemed outside of your parent's control caused your parent to act in a way that was very destructive to all involved.

When composing this letter, try very hard to put yourself in your parent's shoes regarding what must have felt like terrible conflicts—for example, conflicts between preservation of memories versus preservation of amicable current relationships, or between saving items in an effort to avoid deprivation versus maintaining living space—and how this has guided your parent's decision making about discarding versus saving items. Try to find forgiveness in your heart for your parent's behaviors, given how desperate he or she must have felt throughout many years of hoarding. The goal is not for your parent to read this letter and be moved to change his or her behavior; rather, this letter is for *you* to find a way to forgive your parent for what you have endured, with insight into your parent's seemingly impossible task of reconciling the need to save with real-life expectations of hospitable living and prioritization of current relationships. Following is an example of a forgiveness letter.

Dear Dad,

I have been doing a lot of reflecting on my life recently, and I've come to a few conclusions about our relationship and my upbringing. I am often angry about the conditions that I had to live in and the sacrifices that I had to make at such a young age. And while I do not condone the behavior that is caused by your disorder, I do recognize that it has been hard for you to do things any differently. I know that it is your disorder that causes your behavior (even if you are not always willing to call it a disorder) and that nothing that you did or didn't do when we were growing up was done out of malice. I accept this, and while I do not condone many of the things that you did to our environment growing up, I understand that there is nothing that either of us can do to correct it at this point. I am ready to move on in my life. My intention is to have the best relationship possible with you. Anyway, I wanted to tell you that I forgive you for the past, which I accept as my history, and I hope that we may be able to have a better relationship going forward. I wish that you too could acknowledge the suffering I have endured.

Love, Stephanie

Whether to actually give the letter to your parent or not is up to you.

You can also reduce your unpleasant emotions by using techniques from cognitive behavioral therapy (CBT). As the name implies, CBT teaches that there are things you can do to change both the way you think (your cognition) and the way you behave.

THE COGNITIVE BEHAVIORAL APPROACH

The cognitive behavioral approach is not necessarily aimed at getting you to "feel better" about everything or indeed anything; rather, it is aimed at allowing you to approach things in a more productive way and with more balanced thinking, thereby allowing real change and improvement to occur in your life. Below, we will describe how you can use the cognitive behavioral approach. There are different strategies within the approach, all of which you may view as tools to fill your "toolbox" for helping you deal with negative emotions. We will also provide you with specific practical exercises, according to the emotional experience that they are intended to target.

As the child of a hoarder, you probably avoid certain situations because they make you uncomfortable or because they bring about unpleasant emotions. For example, you may avoid reaching out to your parent who hoards, because the state of your parent's home depresses you. This "avoidance behavior" allows you to avoid the emotional discomfort of being exposed to the clutter. CBT teaches that although it is natural to want to run away from situations that make you feel bad, in the long run this behavior does not help you deal with the realities of your life. If you avoid reaching out to your parent, for example, in the long run you may not really have much of a relationship with your parent. The cognitive behavioral approach teaches you to confront situations that you are avoiding because they make you uncomfortable so that you can live a fuller and happier life.

Let's say that Stephanie finds it very difficult to even enter her father's home and stand amid the clutter. The squalid conditions cause her to have an extreme disgust reaction, which causes her father to feel embarrassed and disrespected. It's okay for Stephanie to feel disgusted and to express to her father that she finds it difficult to enter the house, or to refuse to do so. However, if she felt she could, or if she needed to—as some children of hoarders do when they attempt to help their parents clean up or move—Stephanie could also engage in some *graded* (i.e., gradual) *exposure* to better prepare herself to enter her father's house and be surrounded by the clutter while managing her feelings of disgust. Graded exposure to disgust-inducing imagery involves slow, progressive contact with that imagery, so as to build tolerance to the feeling. We will elaborate on how to do graded exposures to disgusting images later in this section. On the other hand, if contact with her father's home proves too difficult, Stephanie could also set boundaries by telling her father that the house is unsafe and unhealthy and that, while she found it difficult to live in the house as a child but had to nevertheless, she prefers not to be exposed to it as an adult.

CBT also involves learning to change your thoughts and your interpretations of situations. As you know, in any given situation we all react differently, and this is because of the way we each view the situation and what we each think. CBT holds that in any situation, the more logical your thinking is, the less negatively you will feel; excessive negative feelings are a result of not thinking logically. Cognitive behavioral therapists ask their clients to challenge the accuracy of troubling thoughts, because sometimes even a strongly held belief is determined to be inaccurate. Once you identify your thought, challenge its logic or accuracy, and find it to be unfounded or exaggerated, then you can begin to behave under a more logical belief system, and likely feel better as a result. Cognitive behavioral strategies may be useful in terms of adjusting your beliefs about your parent and finding redeemable aspects of your relationship with your parent.

If Stephanie is too angry and resentful about her father's hoarding to understand it as the condition that it is—she says things like "My dad is the most selfish man; he never cared about how the hoarding situation made us feel. He only ever demonstrated affection for his things!"—cognitive behavioral strategies could give Stephanie opportunities to examine the accuracy of some of her thoughts. A cognitive behavioral therapist might use the following line of questioning with Stephanie: "What is the evidence that he never cared about you? What is the evidence that he did care? Is it accurate to say that he never demonstrated affection? Can you think of any examples of him demonstrating affection?" Eventually Stephanie would learn to question her own thoughts as they arose, to try to distinguish her father's hoarding behaviors from his feelings about his family.

A form of CBT that we discussed in chapter 4 is acceptance and commitment therapy (ACT), which is another tool for your "toolbox." As a review, remember that you are encouraged to experience negative feelings rather than run away from them and to direct your life according to your values. Do what you need to do despite feeling angry, depressed, or disgusted. Do not let your emotions rule you.

Below, you will find specific exercises to manage your day-to-day struggles associated with the emotional impact of hoarding. We will delve into how specific emotions manifest in the lives of children of hoarders, and we will provide specific therapeutic techniques that will aid you in managing those feelings.

COPING WITH PAIN, FRUSTRATION, ANGER, AND RESENTMENT THROUGH EXPOSURE AND "BARBING"

Children of hoarders commonly feel pain, frustration, and anger: anger about their living conditions; pain in the repeated prioritization of material items over relationships, and frustration about their parent's unwillingness to confront the problem. These negative emotions tend to be insidious ones that cause people to communicate in hostile and aggressive ways. Regardless of what the frustration or anger is directed toward, knee-jerk (or nondeliberate) expression of your anger can result in its perpetuation and a lack of progress with regard to the goal of a healthier lifestyle for your parent, possibly leading to estrangement. So, below, we propose a few techniques aimed at minimizing the damaging effects of pain and anger.

Barbing is a therapeutic technique that basically involves confronting things that provoke your frustration, pain, and anger yet deliberately responding without aggression or hostility. The purpose of barbing yourself is to practice sitting with ideas—thoughts, images, and things that people might say—that inspire emotions like frustration and anger, and refraining from acting in an unproductive way. Because of its potential to make you extremely angry, barbing is an exercise that you should plan carefully and perform slowly, in your own time. Below, we present the steps of constructing an anger hierarchy. Afterward, we will elaborate on the process of exposure to (getting used to) the items on the hierarchy.

Exercise: Compose an Anger Hierarchy

Ask yourself what makes you most angry about your parent's living situation and its impact on you. Identify three anger-provoking thoughts: thought 1, thought 2, and thought 3. Jot them down in a notebook or on a separate piece of paper.

Now identify imagery that inspires your anger about your parent's hoarding. You can focus on images in your memory—perhaps of events that led you to feel embarrassed, ashamed, or resentful of your parent. You can also focus on areas of your parent's home that make you particularly angry. Identify three anger-provoking images: image 1, image 2, and image 3. It may be helpful to photograph specific areas of your parent's home so that you can have these images in front of you. It may also be useful to write detailed descriptions of the images in your memory and the events surrounding them, so you can have this in front of you as well.

Now identify things that your parent might say to you that would cause you to feel resentment, frustration, alienation, and disbelief. What has your parent said in the past that caused you to feel this way? Identify three anger-provoking expressions: expression 1, expression 2, and expression 3. Write them down.

Now assign each thought, image, or expression a number on a scale of 1 to 10 to indicate the degree of anger that you feel surrounding it, where 1 indicates little anger and 10 indicates extreme anger. More than one item can have the same number. Then list the items by category, in order of most anger provoking to least anger provoking.

		Anger (1–10)
Thoughts	1.	
	2.	
	3.	
Images	1.	
	2.	
	3.	
Expressions	1.	
	2.	
	3.	

The items with lower numbers in your hierarchy are the ones that you will want to start with when planning a barbing regimen. It is advised that you work from the least difficult to the most difficult item on your list. During barbing, you will sit with each thought, image, or expression until you no longer feel the urge to respond in an aggressive or hostile manner. You can enlist the help of a neutral third party—perhaps a trusted friend or sibling—to coach you through the exposure and prompt you to remain productive about your response to your feelings. Throughout all barbing exercises, be sure to refrain from acting out in an angry way (yelling, expressing hostility, etc.). Following are the steps in the barbing procedure.

Before you actually expose yourself to the thought, image, or expression that angers you:

1. Bring to mind the thoughts, feelings, and images surrounding what you will be exposing yourself to.

2. Sit with the anger, frustration, and desperation that may arise.

3. Bring to mind what your frustration and anger normally urge you to do in this and similar situations. Remind yourself to be willing to tolerate the feelings that accompany this imagery.

If you are exposing yourself to an anger-provoking image, next look at your pictures depicting the scenario that triggers your anger, or imagine the scene in as much detail as possible, as if you were actually in the situation. Practice sitting with these thoughts with mindful awareness (explained in chapter 4). After you have done this several times, you will likely notice feelings of boredom during exposure to this particular image. This is how you will know that the exposure is working to reduce your anger. The number of times required to give you this relief is uncertain, and it varies from person to person, but the likelihood is that after the fourth or fifth time, you will start to notice a shift or reduction in your anger.

You can follow a similar procedure for an anger-provoking thought or unproductive mantra that may repeat in your mind. If the thought is something to the effect of *I can't believe that she would choose things over her family*, practice sitting with this thought, and continue to try to tap into the emotion underlying it. Repeat this until the emotion itself becomes less distressing. As a general rule, you should practice exposure exercises daily when you are initially habituating to a new source of discomfort.

If the item from your anger hierarchy that you are exposing yourself to is something your parent might say, first engage in a mindfulness sitting meditation, such as the one described in chapter 4. In as much detail as you can, imagine your parent saying the words over and over again; it is expected that you will feel some anger as you do this. Repeat until you notice that you are more bored than angry. The second phase of exposing yourself to something your parent might say involves hearing the words being said to you. For this task, ask someone whom you trust to assist you. Tell the person who is aiding you in this exercise to repeat the words as though your parent was speaking them to you. If your parent has said or would say these words in anger, instruct your assistant to use an angry tone. As your assistant speaks the words, close your eyes and imagine that your parent is speaking the words to you. Or, if it makes you angrier to watch your assistant's face, do so. Continue with the repetition of the expression, until, again, you feel boredom rather than anger.

Over time, we recommend that you use the above procedure with the items on your hierarchy that you rated as highly anger provoking. Go at a pace that feels challenging, but not overwhelming. The goal is not to gain complete relief from the anger that you feel surrounding these thoughts, images, and expressions, but rather to gain exposure to the experience of being angry. This practice will empower you to experience anger without necessarily becoming drawn into angry behavior. If you are prepared to experience anger-provoking scenarios, with resolve to act in opposition to the feelings that these scenarios might evoke, you are on the road to acting in line with who you would like to be, rather than who your angry impulses will urge you to be.

COPING WITH DEPRESSION THROUGH BEHAVIORAL ACTIVATION

Depression is very commonly experienced by children of hoarders. This is completely logical, since depression is often associated with feelings of hopelessness and helplessness; given the unchanging nature of your situation, it is understandable that you would feel both helpless and hopeless. Depressed feelings can cause a range of unpleasant experiences that have far-reaching effects on your functioning. Depression is known to cause behavioral inhibition, or inactivity, and loss of interest in things that you found enjoyable in the past. Below, we will discuss a therapeutic technique referred to as "behavioral activation." And, later, we will revisit committed action (introduced in chapter 4) as a way of enriching your life.

To put this procedure very simply, behavioral activation represents the "just do it" approach to a problem. If there is something that you know you should be doing or that you have been dreading doing, and you are not doing it primarily due to (a) lack of energy, (b) a feeling that you "can't be bothered," or (c) feelings of not caring about "anything," behavioral activation may be a very useful strategy for you. Behavioral activation predominantly involves identifying things that need to be done, determining the most appropriate ways of accomplishing these tasks, and breaking each task down in a step-by-step manner.

You may wonder how accomplishing tasks will allow you to experience some relief from your depression. Basically, the way it works is twofold: (1) taking care of your responsibilities helps you feel less overwhelmed, which can improve your mood, and (2) behavioral activation applies not only to stressful responsibilities, but also to enjoyable experiences. As we mentioned, depression can sometimes cause a lack of interest in things that once inspired you. Therefore, you can also use behavioral activation to reinvest

103

yourself in activities that you once loved. In fact, some studies have found that behavioral activation can be as effective as antidepressant medications (Martell, Dimidjian, and Herman-Dunn 2010).

Exercise: Generate a Behavioral-Activation Schedule

The aim of this exercise is to determine (a) your most pressing tasks or responsibilities, (b) things you used to enjoy that you no longer do, and (c) what stands in the way of accomplishing each of these things.

In a notebook or on a separate sheet of paper, generate a list of responsibilities that you have neglected, both related to your parent's hoarding and otherwise. For example, are there bills that you need to pay? Have you been putting off taking the car in for an inspection? Make the list long and comprehensive; break each item down in terms of its constituent tasks. Do not become overwhelmed by the length of the list. The purpose of this part of the process is to look at *everything* in your life that requires your attention and to prioritize the most pressing tasks. Once you have completed your list, put a star next to activities that must be completed before the end of the day, put a dash next to activities that must be completed by the end of the week, put a bullet point next to activities that must be completed within the next month, and put a heart next to items or activities that you have enjoyed and would like to reincorporate into your routine.

The next step is to plan the next twenty-four hours with attention to the list you generated. What needs to be accomplished in the next day, and when can you accomplish it? Write an hour-by-hour schedule, and be sure to include at least one enjoyable (or previously enjoyable) activity.

Complete a similar schedule for the week, but focus more on what you need to accomplish throughout the week and what day you plan to do what. At this point, there is no need to complete an hour-by-hour schedule for the week—just provide a rough schedule of what needs to be done on what day. Following this, complete a schedule for the month. Schedule certain activities throughout the month that are aimed not only at confronting responsibilities, but also at getting reinvolved in all the things in life that have meaning to you or that you enjoy. This should give you a rough outline of how you would like to proceed in the longer term.

As you complete the activities you have planned, it is likely that you will experience some relief from feelings of depression, because activity and productivity can be immensely powerful in this regard. Having a plan alone can serve as motivation for moving forward, but if you struggle in the moment to complete any specific task, try the next exercise.

Exercise: Motivation for Task Completion

Bring to mind the activity that you struggle to find motivation to complete. Let us say, for example, that you are having difficulty cleaning your home. Cleaning your home may seem to be an overwhelming task on the whole, and that may cause you to want to avoid it completely, especially if you are experiencing depressive symptoms. Instead of looking at the whole house, identify one task that needs to be completed—washing the dishes, for example. Ask yourself whether you can wash all the dirty dishes. If you feel as though you could not wash all the dishes, then resolve to wash just one dish. Washing one dish should not take you more than thirty seconds; this certainly you can tolerate. Wash one dish, and then ask yourself whether you can wash another (another thirty-second commitment). When this is done, ask yourself whether you can continue to take one dish at a time, not becoming overwhelmed by the stack of dishes that ultimately need to be washed; just washing one at a time.

This exercise is intended to demonstrate that any task can appear less overwhelming if it is deconstructed and presented in palatable individual tasks. Most everything in life can be approached in this way. And as you realize that each individual task is manageable, you will begin to chip away at everything that appeared overwhelming at first glance.

COPING WITH DISGUST THROUGH EXPOSURE

Disgust for the state of your parent's home may make it difficult for you to interact with your parent who hoards and will certainly make you feel disgusted at the thought of going through the clutter. This is completely understandable. A home full of clutter can be quite disgusting, especially considering some of the environmental conditions that we explored in chapter 2. If you are sensitive or easily disgusted, it is likely that you have difficulty being around your parent and your parent's home, in particular. The exposure process below is intended to help you manage some of your feelings of disgust while pursuing a life that you value (which may involve being in your parent's home—especially if your parent agrees, at some point, to a group cleanup effort). The format of the exercise will follow the format of the anger hierarchy exercise. Again, the aim is not to remove your feelings of disgust for things that are objectively disgusting, but rather to allow you to tolerate feelings of disgust while following an action that is important to the life that you want for yourself.

When proceeding with an exposure agenda, with the aim of becoming somewhat desensitized to the disgusting things that you will encounter in your parent's home, it is important to first generate a list of images that you have encountered within your parent's home, as well as thoughts that you have about the overall disgusting conditions of the home.

Exercise: Construct a Hierarchy of Feelings of Disgust

On a separate sheet, write a detailed list of up to ten things in your parent's home that cause you to feel disgust. Examples are cockroaches, mice (and mouse feces), fly infestations (and associated maggots), evidence of animal urine and feces, spoiled food and other decomposing organic material, evidence of your parent's poor hygiene, and the presence of used diapers or other visible human waste. With all of these images, there will be an accompanying odor for you to imagine as well. It is important that you use *all* your senses to imagine what disgusts you that you might encounter in your parent's home when making this list.

Assign each image a number from 1 to 10, with 1 indicating slightly disgusting and 10 indicating the most disgusting thing that you will encounter in your parent's home. More than one image can have the same number. Then list the images in order of most disgusting to least disgusting.

Image	Disgust (1–10)
1.	
2.	
3.	
4.	
5.	
6.	
7.	
8.	
9.	
10.	

The next step is preparing for exposure exercises. For example, if you listed spoiled food in the refrigerator, begin with a photograph of spoiled food in a refrigerator (which you can find on the Internet). Look at the photo until your disgust reaction begins to subside; then find another image that is similarly disgusting, and look at it until your disgust reaction subsides. Continue with this practice on a daily basis until these images trigger less of a disgust reaction overall than they once did. Then proceed to observing actual spoiled food, whether in your own home or in your parent's home. Become acquainted with what exactly it is about the spoiled food (or whatever disgusts you) that makes you feel disgusted. Maybe it is the smell; maybe it is the sight of mold and other growth. Continue to expose yourself to this imagery until it no longer causes you to have such a visceral disgust reaction.

Repeat this process for other items on your hierarchy. The aim here is to become comfortable enough with the images to be able to function in your parent's home, should you have to be there for any value-driven reason (e.g., helping clean up).

SUMMARY

This chapter provided you with skills, techniques, exercises, and "tools" from the cognitive behavioral approach that will enable you to function more comfortably among the conditions of your parent's home. The exercises in this chapter were aimed at common psychological struggles of children of hoarders, including struggles with pain, anger, depression, and disgust. We explored forgiveness, barbing, behavioral activation, and exposure to disgusting imagery. In the following chapters, we will examine how you can use these tools in order to manage your day-to-day struggles as a child of a hoarder.

CHAPTER 6

Improving Your Relationship with Your Parent

I want to stop fighting with my dad about the hoarding situation. I want to find a way to continue our relationship even though my dad keeps hoarding. I believe that my intentions are good. I really don't want to just take a shot at my dad or upset him about the hoarding, but somehow we always end up fighting about the state of his house. I want to break the pattern. I know that my dad's hoarding is not going to magically lift, and I have finally decided that I don't want to sacrifice my relationship with my dad, squandering our relationship in his final years. I need to find a way to do this, but it is so hard to break the pattern.

—Daniel

In chapter 4, we introduced acceptance and commitment therapy (ACT), and we elaborated on the concepts behind the ACT approach to behavior change. You did some exercises in which you practiced using the ACT skills of willingness, mindfulness, cognitive defusion, values clarification, and committed action. In this chapter, we are going to ask you to put those skills to use to improve your relationship with your parent who hoards. We want to help you have better interactions with your parent, curtail any of your behaviors that are enabling your parent's hoarding, and hopefully see your parent as not just a hoarder but someone with many good qualities as well. We will ask you to reflect on the values-clarification exercise in chapter 4 and then ask you to make a commitment to live according to your values, especially with regard to your relationship with your parent who hoards. The aim of this chapter is not to fix the problem or to help your parent enact lasting change. Rather, we are going to ask you to find a balance in which both your and your parent's basic wants are met, which will work in terms of improving the character of your relationship.

Look back at your "Importance" and "Success" ratings for the area of "Other Family Relationships" in the values-clarification exercise in chapter 4 and think about how your relationship with your parent who hoards fits in this category. Did your relationship with your parent influence your ratings? How successful do you feel in your relationship with your parent who hoards? You may have very ambivalent feelings about your success in this area. Maybe you feel as though you have done everything that you can for your parent, and therefore you should feel successful, but your relationship with your parent is still tense. On the other hand, you may feel as though overall your relationship with your parent is good, but perhaps it is fair to say that your approach to the relationship is ultimately hurtful to both of you and to the relationship. If for many years you have urged your parent to get treatment or to agree to clean up the mess; if you have fought endlessly with your parent; if you have given up, isolating yourself from your parent completely;

or if you have given in, avoiding conflict entirely while watching the hoarding worsen, this has likely made a big difference in how successful you believe you have been in maintaining a good relationship with your parent. Perhaps conflict in your relationship with your parent seems unavoidable, and this contributes to a sense of failure. But avoidance of conflict is not necessarily the mark of a healthy or successful relationship either.

Given the complex circumstances and dynamics involved, it is easy to see how assigning a number to your success in having a relationship with your parent who hoards is complicated. In this sense, we ask that you carefully examine what your goals are, as far as your relationship with your parent. Your goals might be different from your parent's goals. For example, while you may have the goal of restoring functionality and safety to your mother's home, she may believe that the conditions of the home are not a problem and that you should accept her for who she is. The most realistic goal probably lies somewhere in between: your mother can accept some responsibility for improving conditions in the home, in order to ensure safety, and you can accept that she sees things differently than you, and needs to be approached and worked with accordingly.

Because you can "help" your parent either in a way that is productive (e.g., using gentle, assertive communication, coupled with firm boundaries) or in a way that is unproductive (e.g., using angry expressions of resentment and hostility or undertaking efforts to reduce or clean up the mess without your parent's consent), we want to impress on you the importance of keeping your values and goals in mind when dealing with your parent's hoarding. But we recognize also that, for some children of hoarders, the exercise below may not be appropriate because you are struggling with estrangement, and you feel you need to be able to distance yourself from the negative relationship. Whatever the case, you need to make your own path. If you are trying to save some part of your relationship with your parent who hoards, the exercise below may help.

Exercise: How You Value Your Relationship with Your Parent

In a notebook or on a separate piece of paper, briefly elaborate on a few ways in which you believe that you demonstrate that you value your relationship with your parent who hoards. Copy the following statement, then write three responses.

I demonstrate that I value my relationship with my parent in the following ways:

1.

2.

3.

Now elaborate on some ways in which you feel as if you fall short of demonstrating how important your relationship with your parent is to you. Copy the following statement, then write three responses.

I fall short in this valued area in the following ways:

1.

2.

3.

Take a look at your responses to this exercise. Are behaviors such as calling your parent, visiting your parent, cleaning up after your parent, and talking about the clutter and the lack of safety in the house examples of how you show that you value your relationship? Are behaviors such as not calling, not inviting your parent to your house, and avoiding the subject of your parent with your children examples of how you do not show that you value your relationship? Perhaps you think that efforts to avoid uncomfortable situations or painful feelings about your parent's hoarding are somehow helpful or noble. Yet as much as you can rationalize these kinds of actions, and as reasonable as your argument for them likely is, it may not actually be what is motivating your approach.

To illustrate this point, when we asked Daniel (who provided the quote with which we opened this chapter) to elaborate on his helpful behaviors with regard to handling his father's hoarding, he indicated that on his weekly visits to his father's home, he would point out things that needed to be done to improve the conditions in the home, and he made efforts to clean up the areas that his father would tolerate to be cleared. While this seems like a helpful approach on paper, when we asked what the outcome of these efforts was, Daniel indicated that typically his father would become defensive. And the areas that were cleared during one visit were often cluttered again when Daniel arrived for his next visit. Not only was Daniel's approach unsuccessful in the long run, but also it caused his father to become increasingly resentful, withdrawn, and distrustful.

Since the efforts that Daniel identified as helpful ultimately made no positive difference, what purpose were these actions actually serving? Avoidance of discomfort provides us with an unwelcome explanation. It might have been that Daniel could not tolerate seeing his father living in squalor; therefore, he spent his time with his father in attempts to reduce the clutter and thus reduce his discomfort. Because his goals differed from his father's goals, he achieved nothing, the relationship suffered, and his father became more withdrawn and unwilling to cooperate with Daniel's efforts to clean up.

Similarly, you may be well intentioned but your efforts may not necessarily create a climate for willing change on your parent's part. For example, when Stephanie discussed with us decisions that she made in hopes of making a difference in her father's hoarding, she reported, "My dad knows that I will not let him see Marisa [his granddaughter] until he bends and lets us start to clean up the house. It is hard to hold this over him, but he has to know that there are consequences for his behavior." While we understand that painful decisions like these may be necessary—Stephanie may be acting to protect her daughter from a potentially toxic environment—we recommend that you resort to such threats and ultimatums only if you fully intend to carry them out, and only if you think that imposing the stated consequence is preferable to allowing things to continue the way they are. In other words, be prepared for the reality that the hoarding situation will not get any better. For example, unless Stephanie thinks that not allowing her father and his granddaughter to ever see each other is really better than permitting occasional visits under the circumstances, she should refrain from suggesting that this may happen. This is because as we mentioned, hoarders are very resistant to change, so the most likely outcome will be that the hoarding behavior will continue.

It's possible that Stephanie did not truly want to cut her father off from his granddaughter permanently if he resisted attempts to clean up. Rather, she may have been so frustrated by the clutter that she just wanted her frustration acknowledged. And Stephanie's decision might have been driven more by emotional avoidance (in this case, not wanting to be continually frustrated) than by her values, which would make it an example of how emotional avoidance can masquerade as a helpful approach to your parent's hoarding.

Even if you feel as if you are helping and acting according to your values, you may actually be satisfying an emotional urge through expressions of negative emotions, however reasonable they may seem. In other words, even if it feels as if you are trying to move in a valued direction by bringing a health or safety issue to your parent's attention, you may actually be upsetting a productive dynamic between you and your parent. In order to ensure that you are not acting at odds with the value of your relationship with your parent, we ask that you carefully examine the motivation for your behavior. *Why* do you want to confront your parent about a particular issue? *Why* do you want to phrase it the way that you have chosen to? Is either of these considerations influenced by frustration, anger, resentment, or other negative emotions?

We ask that you balance your value-oriented behaviors between asserting boundaries on one hand and ensuring that your parent's basic health and safety needs are met on the other. These goals are sometimes at odds with each other. Likewise, you will have to find the delicate balance between involvement in and detachment from the problem of your parent's hoarding. The "right" answer when dealing with your parent who hoards varies based on circumstances. Through the techniques explored below, we hope to bring some clarity to the process of finding a system that works for you, while keeping your values in mind.

VALUING YOUR PARENT, YOURSELF, AND YOUR RELATIONSHIP

It is important to note, again, that some children of hoarders choose to have a relationship with their parent, and others do not. There are many reasons for the choices one makes: the severity of the hoarding, the normalcy of the parent's behavior outside of the hoarding situation, the extent to which the parent validated their child's feelings and frustrations, the developmental stage at which the child was exposed to the hoarding, and whether or not there were any adults who protected the child and made him or her feel wanted, respected, loved, and secure.

If you find yourself able to value your relationship with your parent despite his or her hoarding behaviors, you have to find a balance between becoming absorbed in the problem of your parent's hoarding on one hand and self-preservation on the other, as well as give attention to other values in your life. No matter how pressing it may be, no one life area should be a "black hole" for all your mental, physical, and emotional resources. This includes your relationship with your parent: it should never absorb all your attention, effort, and energy. Recall the discussion of values in chapter 4. It is typical to have a variety of valued life areas, and it is healthy to give attention to each area according to how important the area is. Therefore, it is a good idea to prioritize your relationship with your parent if you value it, but do not neglect other valued areas in the process. Balancing your wants with what is best for your relationship with your parent involves careful examination of your desires, careful examination of your parent's desires, and finding a mutually agreeable compromise.

Exercise: What Your Parent Wants/How Are Your Interests at Odds with This?

This exercise is aimed at distilling how your parent's wants may be at odds with your own. A typical clash of interests, which appears clear-cut and without much emotional impact, is as follows: your mother wants not to be questioned about how much cleaning she got done over the past week, and you want her to clean pretty consistently. How are these at odds with each other? Well, your mother probably does not want to be questioned because she is having a hard time disposing of things, and you want her to be accountable for the cleanup so that it gets done. Of course, cleanup is not the only possible area of conflict with your parent who hoards—you and your parent could clash over how frequently or infrequently you invite your parent over, the tone and nature of telephone calls, the need and time frame to have broken appliances repaired, other home improvement or maintenance issues, or any number of things.

In a notebook or on a separate piece of paper, list some-thing that your parent wants or requests with regard to the hoarding and then list what you would like to happen. We will then ask you to examine how your interests may be at odds with your parent's.

For example:

Your parent requests: *To be left to his own devices; that you have sensitivity for what he is going through; that you have patience, accept things as they are, and remain involved in his life*

You would like: *Not to feel as though I am a hostage to the hoarding situation; to be validated for my suffering over the years; acknowledgement of what I have gone through; an apology; to ensure my dad's safety; to ensure the safety of my children when they are in his home*

Because it is not healthy to pour all your energy into one valued life area, there are times when you will benefit from accepting an impasse when your wants are at odds with your parent's. However, the exercise above also highlights an opportunity to employ *behavioral contracting*, or coming up with an acceptable arrangement. Assuming that your relationship with your parent would allow for compromise, showing some behavioral flexibility lays a good foundation for a collaborative, rather than coercive, approach. So referring to the above example, you might point out that it is impossible for your desire for safety within your father's home to be met so long as your father insists on being "left to his own devices." The two just do not mesh. If your father wants you to have patience to remain involved in his life, your requests for his health and safety must be met on some level. A compromise needs to be made. Maybe his request to be "left to his own devices" can be better clarified; maybe he does not want you to constantly bring up the subject of his hoarding? Maybe he does not want to feel judged and belittled due to the condition of his home? If either of these would help satisfy his desire to be "left to his own devices," these can be reasonable requests to include in a behavioral contract. Specifically, your father can ask you to limit confronting him about his hoarding, to refrain from judgmental statements, and so on. If you are able to do this, would your father be willing to meet your requests for improvements in safety within the home? Would he be able to ensure safe passage to important areas within the home and make efforts to limit squalor or infestation?

Exercise: Draft a Behavioral Contract

With the previous exercise in mind, can you think of reasonable terms for a behavioral contract between you and your parent? Remember, the goal here is collaborating with your parent on a mutually tolerable agreement. Generate a few offers and counteroffers to present to your parent regarding to contentious issues between you.

Issue 1

Your offer to your parent:

_____

_____

Your request of your parent:

_____

_____

Issue 2

Your offer to your parent:

_____

_____

Your request of your parent:

_____

_____

Issue 3

Your offer to your parent:

_____

_____

Your request of your parent:

_____

_____

You may be saying, "I have tried to negotiate, and my father doesn't keep his end of the bargain. I am tired of being disappointed and facing false promises." If attempts to draft a contract fail once or twice, we ask that you try again. However, if you feel that negotiation is impossible, you may have to adjust the strategy we have just described to fit the kind of relationship, if any, that you decide you and your parent can have. And, if you are living in the house and conditions become unbearable, it's okay to focus on getting out of it as soon as possible. Find a friend or family member to help you do this.

MINDFUL COMMUNICATION

As we discussed in chapter 4, mindfulness relates to present-moment awareness of your experiences and deliberate attention to how you manage your reactions. Mindfulness can be immensely useful in improving the character of your relationship with your parent who hoards.

Mindfulness is all about having the reins and knowing *why* you are approaching a situation the way that you are approaching it. For this reason, mindful communication is often careful and purposeful. We will ask you to look at the purpose of everything that comes out of your mouth when you are speaking to your parent, especially as it relates to sensitive topics.

As we briefly explored above, your approach to your parent's hoarding may be motivated not by your values but by either negative feelings or an unwillingness to have them—and thus not truly helpful. For example, expressing hostility toward your parent can sometimes feel noble, because you are "telling it like it is," "cutting the BS," being direct, speaking frankly, or whatever you wish to call it. The reality, however, is that you are frustrated, annoyed, angry, embarrassed, or fed up. This approach is flawed for two reasons: you are assuming (a) that your parent can be compelled to interpret the situation as you do and (b) that to do so would leave your parent with no choice but to change. Neither of these assumptions typically holds up with hoarders. Hoarding and the mind-set that accompanies it are notoriously rigid, and even if a hoarder can and does acknowledge the problem, there is no guarantee of change, due to how reinforcing (see chapter 1) hoarding behavior is for the hoarder. Rather, communication of hostility will likely lead to further rigidity, with your parent "digging in" even more. Perhaps as illustrated in the examples of Tim in chapter 1 and Angela's mother in chapter 3, your parent will believe *you* to be the problem, rather than the hoarding situation. This pattern plays out in many psychological disorders: when a person with a disorder feels coerced to change, the person is likely to feel alienated from the very people who might serve as sources of support and to retreat even further into disordered behavior.

So what is the alternative in this example? As we discussed in chapter 3, assertive communication and validation may be more productive than hostility and aggression. The use of mindfulness in this context is integral. Because it is so easy to slip back into aggressive or hostile communication patterns, staying with a productive communication style takes constant present-moment redirection. When you are in conversation with your parent who hoards, and you begin to feel as though you are approaching an impasse or an obstacle, keep these questions in mind: "What is my purpose in saying what I am about to say? Is it in line with my goals and values in this situation? Or is it in service of my own emotional urges?" The exercise below is intended to provide you with a mindful way to approach conversations with your parent. Practicing mindful attention during conversations with your parent will enable you to keep the dialogue productive—and value-driven—rather than emotionally reactive. Obviously, it will not be possible for you to use mindfulness during *every* interaction, but we recommend that you use it when the conversation involves sensitive topics, such as in the behavioral-contracting exercise discussed above. The emphasis here is on practicing purposeful, functional statements aimed at finding a compromise.

Do you recall the sitting meditation from chapter 4? Breathing and sitting are only two of countless activities that can be done with mindful attention. Meditation practice can be extended to just about every human activity, including eating, walking, driving, and even interacting. We ask that you carry out the following exercise at a time when you are with your parent and are prepared to talk about sensitive topics.

Exercise: A Mindful Conversation with Your Parent

Sit comfortably, and take a minute to observe any sensations, feelings, or thoughts that jump out at you. What is the first physical sensation that you notice? Acknowledge the sensation, without doing anything to change it. What is the best word to describe your immediate feelings? Acknowledge the emotion, without trying to change it or struggle against it. Just let it be there. Now acknowledge the first thought that occurs to you. Do not try to argue with it or evaluate it. Just acknowledge it, then let it go.

Now turn your attention to your parent. Reflect on your parent mindfully, observing any thoughts or feelings that come up. Notice emotionally loaded observations (e.g., "Mom is so stubborn"), as well as innocuous observations (e.g., "Mom got a haircut"). Do not mull over any one particular thought or feeling, no matter how urgent or awful it seems to you.

As you proceed with the conversation, acknowledge whatever you observe and then let it go. Your overarching strategy during this conversation will be to slow things down, reflect on how you are feeling throughout the interaction, and choose how to respond based on what would be the best and most productive approach. Do not fear the unpleasant feelings that may arise during your conversation, knowing that you have control of your behavior and can choose the useful and helpful approach, rather than the emotionally guided one. When your parent makes a statement, reflect on how it makes you feel and what would be the most productive response, keeping in mind the communication skills we discussed in chapter 3. *Slow down* and tell yourself not to react until you have decided how to act deliberately. Check in with yourself periodically as to how you are feeling throughout the conversation. Every five minutes or so, purposefully practice mindful awareness of sensations, feelings, and thoughts, with an emphasis on letting these experiences go. When you feel the pull of an emotionally guided response, gently acknowledge it and determine what would be a productive, value-driven alternative. If you find that you have been carried away from the task of mindfulness, do not chastise yourself for this; it is human nature to resist present-moment focus and reduction in emotional reactivity. Instead gently guide yourself back to the task.

Afterward, reflect on your experience and what it was like for you to practice mindful conversation. Did any particular thought or feeling pull you off course? Did anything that your parent said cause you to lose sight of the exercise and urge you to respond emotionally? If so, this does not mean that the exercise was a failure. Rather, you now have valuable information as to what triggers mindless (automatic) responses and emotional reactivity in you. This information will help you develop better mindfulness skills for future conversations.

DEFUSING LABELS AND ROLES IN YOUR RELATIONSHIP WITH YOUR PARENT

In chapter 4, we introduced the concept of cognitive defusion as a means of developing a healthier relationship with nagging or distressing thoughts. We focused on defusing thoughts and not immediately buying into them as an alternative to believing them "whole hog." This has special significance in your situation, because many of your thoughts probably revolve around your experience as the child of a hoarder, and many of your thoughts about your parent probably involve the "hoarder" label. When you feel tethered to the label "child of a hoarder," it is hard to view yourself in any other terms, and once you have mentally assigned the label "hoarder" to your parent, you are unlikely to view your parent as anything else either.

Labels may be useful to a discussion such as ours because they describe people's roles or certain aspects of their lives, but the problem with labels is that when you buy into them, it becomes very hard not to act in accordance with them, even though labels cannot fully describe you, your parent, or anyone else as a person. Therefore, if you are totally "fused" with (see chapter 4) and emotionally invested in labels—both those that you assign to your parent (e.g., "hoarder," "stubborn," "inconsiderate") and those that you assign to yourself (e.g., "helpless," "resentful," "hopeless")—it limits your ability to see other aspects of yourself and your parent. Furthermore, it limits your behavior to those behaviors that are in line with your labels. In other words, it creates a self-fulfilling prophecy.

It is important to remember that both you and your parent possess countless characteristics and fulfill a variety of roles. None of the unpleasant labels that you assign to either your parent or yourself can possibly capture all your many qualities. It is easy to define a thing by its flaws, as the negatives tend to jump out at you; it is often harder to notice the positives, but that does not mean that there are none or that they are less important. If you are able to defuse some of these labels, you will open yourself up to a broader range of behaviors, unrestricted by these definitions. Remember, "hoarder" is just a word; the thought that your parent is a hoarder is just a thought. You do not need to be dominated by this thought or the feelings surrounding it, regardless of whether it is an accurate statement. Furthermore, you can see your thoughts and your reflections on your parent as "just thoughts," rather than urgent information to be immediately acted upon. Just observe your feelings and thoughts and let them float away. You do not need to attend to every thought or feeling or take action every time you have a thought or feeling. Observation alone is sufficient at times.

Exercise: "I'm Having the Thought That..."

You can do this meditation/free-association exercise (adapted from Hayes and Smith 2005) either out loud or in your head. The benefit of doing it out loud is that you are less vulnerable to being carried away by your thoughts. However, doing it mentally provides you with opportunity to practice mindful redirection of your thoughts when you notice that they have wandered, so either way is fine.

Set aside about ten or fifteen minutes for this meditation. Find a quiet place, get comfortable, and close your eyes. When you are ready to begin, pick a label or a way that you typically see your parent that relates to your parent's hoarding. Watch your thoughts with present-moment focus, as in the "Leaves in a Stream" meditation in chapter 4, while staying on the topic of your parent's hoarding and the labels that you place on his or her traits and behaviors. However, in this exercise, we ask that, as you note your observations either silently or out loud, you begin with the phrase "I'm having the thought that...," and then state the thought. This allows you to recognize the difference between the thought that you are having and the "you" who is having it (see the "Observer Self" meditation in chapter 4). Again, you are creating a distinction between you and your thoughts, reinforcing your autonomy during thoughts about difficult subjects.

Really embrace any relevant thought that you have during this time, and allow yourself to experience any emotions that accompany a thought. Remember to preface each thought with "I'm having the thought that...," creating a distinction between you and your thoughts. And of course, if you notice that your attention has been carried away from the exercise, just gently redirect your focus back to the activity, with mindful attention.

Afterward, reflect on your experience. Did you experience the same emotional struggle as you typically do when considering this topic? Did prefacing your thoughts with "I'm having the thought that..." allow you any awareness of the labels that you impose? Cognitive defusion exercises aimed at minimizing attachment to labels, such as the next one, may allow you to see your parent in a healthier, more balanced light.

ACT warns against overemphasis on labels. It may be tempting to apply the label of "hoarder" as an all-encompassing category for your parent's behavior and for your parent as a whole (after all, we use this label to refer to people like your parent in this book!). But it is important that this word not be synonymous with your parent in your mind.

Exercise: List Your Parent's Roles

Consider the variety of roles that your parent has fulfilled in his or her life. "Roles" may refer to jobs that your parent has had, qualities that your parent was known for, your parent's relationships with other people, and responsibilities that your parent attended to during your formative years, among others. For this exercise, we ask that you reflect on aspects of your parent's persona that do not relate to hoarding. In a notebook or on a separate piece of paper, list these roles, or write a descriptive summary of your parent's character, examining the various other aspects of your parent besides the hoarding behavior. Remember that the goal of this exercise is to consider your parent as a whole and to view your parent's hoarding behavior in the context of his or her other characteristics.

Keep this exercise in mind when you consider valuing your relationship with your parent, as well as what you are valuing. It is easy to dismiss the value of your relationship with your parent when you are thinking of your parent only as a "hoarder." Keeping your parent's other qualities in mind, as well as the knowledge that none of these roles or qualities defines who your parent *is*, may help you treat your parent with compassion and follow a course of committed action.

SUMMARY

In this chapter, we explored ways to improve your relationship with your parent who hoards. You may not necessarily be able to improve the state of your parent's home, but you can manage your emotions about the situation and pursue a healthier relationship dynamic through the use of strategies derived from acceptance and commitment therapy (ACT). We examined the use of values clarification, committed action, mindfulness, and cognitive defusion for pursuing more productive interactions with your parent.

CHAPTER 7

Talking to Others about the Problem

Your parent's hoarding has likely caused you a lot of ongoing stress. You may be worried and preoccupied with the safety and health of your parent (and that of anyone else in the home as well). You may spend a lot of time thinking about the problem and strategizing how to improve your parent's living conditions. You may envision worst-case scenarios involving eviction notices, infestations, accidents, illnesses due to molds or poor air quality, fire-department citations, or town-hall meetings in which the discussion centers on the need to do something about the clutter on your parent's property. Even if these situations are in fact welcome ones for the fact that they start a discussion you thought would be impossible to have, as they are for many children of hoarders, they can represent additional stresses for you: having to deal with your parent's upset responses to perceived disruptions, or having to bail them out of the financial obligations that can crop up in such circumstances. Maybe one or more of these things has already happened, but even just imagining them may have caused you sleepless nights, stomachaches, heart palpitations, or fatigue. You may be depressed, anxious, and angry. If you live with your parent or spend significant time in your parent's home, dealing with the realities of a home full of clutter—from the everyday inconveniences to the safety hazards and health risks—can wreak havoc on your body and mind as well. We would like you to take a moment right now to take stock of your health in some important ways.

Exercise: Assess Your Emotional and Physical Health

List three ways you think your emotional well-being may be suffering due to your parent's hoarding. For example, do you have insomnia? Do you often feel impatient or angry? Is it difficult for you to find joy in anything?

1.

2.

3.

Now list three ways you think your physical well-being may be suffering due to your parent's hoarding. For example, do you often feel fatigued? Do you have frequent headaches or muscle aches?

1.

2.

3.

If you notice that your parent's hoarding is having negative consequences on your emotional and physical well-being, then you need to attend to these things. Attending to your well-being means eating well, sleeping well, and using the strategies we mentioned in previous chapters: cognitive defusion, mindfulness, behavioral contracting, and engagement in behaviors that are conducive to a good relationship. It also requires that you not try to force change on someone who is not motivated or is unable to change.

In the exercise above, you probably identified some ways in which your parent's hoarding is harming your health or contributing to chronic problems. Keeping your struggles and your parent's hoarding a secret—as you may have done for many years—will only negatively affect your physical and emotional well-being even further. This is because holding back thoughts, feelings, or behaviors is associated with long-term stress and disease (e.g., heart disease), as well as impaired immune system functioning (Pennebaker, Kiecolt-Glaser, and Glaser 1988). Sharing your pain with others is thus one way to combat stress and boost your immune system. Both talking to others directly and expressing your feelings in writing have been shown to have benefits for physical and psychological health (Baikie and Wilhelm 2005).

Many different associations exist to help people feel supported in dealing with their problems. You may have heard of Alcoholics Anonymous, Narcotics Anonymous, Overeaters Anonymous, the Diabetic Association, the American Heart Association, and the International Obsessive Compulsive Foundation. At the time of this writing, there is no national organization specifically for hoarding, and in-person support groups for children of hoarders can be hard to find. However, Children of Hoarders (www.childrenof hoarders.com) is an online organization—the first of its kind, established in 2006—whose mission is to address the needs of these children. (For more online resources, see the Resources list in the back of this book.) And many people also have gotten to know about hoarding through television shows, books, and other media. If you were to share your suffering—your feelings about and reactions to your parent's hoarding, as well as the difficulty of wanting to help and not being able to—you might receive understanding, validation, and support.

TO SHARE OR NOT TO SHARE

There is a theory in psychology that self-disclosure leads to disclosure in others. In other words, if you share something about yourself, others are more likely to share something about themselves, and self-disclosure leads to increased feelings of closeness among the people involved (Dindia 2000). This does not mean, however, that you should reveal intimate details about yourself to strangers in an effort to make as many friends as possible. You need to know to whom to disclose and to whom not to disclose. You will need to imagine and examine the possible consequences of disclosing your family's circumstances to this person or that person. And how and also what you reveal is important; if you are not met with understanding, your self-worth may diminish and you may even feel worse. You will need to use judgment in terms of what exactly you disclose.

So let us look at the pros and cons of telling a friend (for example) about your parent's hoarding. Here are some possible pros:

You may feel relieved to tell your secret.

Your friend may also have a hoarder in the family and you will not feel alone in your struggles.

You may enlarge your support system.

Your friend may have thought that you were hiding a bigger problem.

Your friend may have suggestions as to how you can deal with the situation.

Your friend may tell you about a new form of treatment for hoarding.

Now, let us examine why you may *not* want to tell a friend (for example) about your parent's hoarding. Here are some possible cons:

You are not able to control whether your friend tells other people.

Your friend (or other people) may not know how to react or support you.

Your friend (or other people) may think that you are dirty or disgusting.

Your friend may pity you.

You may lose your friend.

Your friend may think that you are at fault for "letting" your parent hoard.

Your friend may trivialize the impact that hoarding has had on your life.

You will need to come up with your own lists of pros and cons and weigh them against each other for each person you consider telling. Although close friends are usually the best choice to share with, perhaps you have thought of telling a colleague, your in-laws, your children, distant relatives, or your parent's neighbor. You may have different pros and cons for each person; thus your decision to share or not to share will not always be the same.

What you decide will also depend on your values. Remember, value-driven action is what you should aim for. Review the life areas you identified as those that you value highly from the values-clarification exercise in chapter 4. Does sharing about your parent's hoarding fit with making progress in your valued life areas or with other values that are important to you, such as honesty? Does it feel okay? For some people it does, and for others it does not. Think about your values, such as privacy, honesty, integrity, loyalty, close relationships, openness with others, or reservedness. Does disclosing to a particular person of your choice fit with these values, or is it against your values? Always act in accordance with your values.

Some people value honesty and openness to the extent that they would decide to tell everyone in their lives. Others value privacy and would tell no one. The best approach, in our opinion, is to value both honesty and privacy and be cautiously trusting of others. Remember to respect not only your privacy but that of other family members, too. Your parents or siblings may not want the family's dirty laundry aired in public. Ask yourself whether your parent has been highly secretive about the hoarding, maybe even trying to keep it a secret from you; this is an indication that your parent's desire for privacy and your desire to gain support or validation may be at odds. The compromise is to carefully select whom you tell. You might share your struggles with your spouse, a friend, or a close relative—someone you trust and who can provide you with support. This is not just your problem—it is both yours and your parent's—so respect your parent's rights too.

Exercise: Whom Will You Tell?

Think of at least three people in your life to whom you have not disclosed your parent's hoarding. If you can, make them different from one another—for example, your supervisor, your neighbor, and your cousin. In a notebook or on a separate piece of paper, write their names and draw up a list of pros and cons of telling each one. Compare your lists and make your decision; write "Tell" or "Not Tell" next to each name.

DO YOU NEED TO LET YOUR PARENT KNOW WHOM YOU ARE GOING TO TELL?

You may be wondering, *Is my parent's hoarding really even my problem to share? Do I have a right to tell people about it?* Just about everyone has the experience of sharing the details of a problem that is not totally theirs at one time or another. The key is how you go about it.

The fact is that your parent's hoarding originated with your parent, but it affects you greatly as well. It probably seems very much like your own problem and a big part of your life. Maybe you are who you are today because you grew up in a home full of clutter. Your parent's hoarding may have exposed you to a host of situations that you were sometimes not ready to deal with, triggered a bunch of emotions that you did not know how to deal with, and molded your personality to some extent.

As we have acknowledged all along, you most likely harbor some resentment and anger toward your parent and the unfairness of your situation. You may want to yell to everyone about what an unfair childhood you had, or you may want to let everyone know how frustrating it is that your mother's house is not fit for human living. Or maybe your need to talk about your parent's hoarding comes from a desire to increase awareness of the impact of hoarding so that others will not have to struggle as you have struggled.

Whatever your motivation, it does not necessarily give you the right to tell everyone, however justifiable your reasons. You do certainly have the right to share how you feel with some people, however.

Making a decision to share about your parent's hoarding carries the same responsibilities as telling someone about any another disorder your parent may have. Hoarding is just getting to be recognized as a psychological disorder, and therefore many people may confuse it with messiness, disorganization, and sloppiness. In reality, it is no different than any other disorder except that it is more readily observable. Anyone who enters a hoarder's home can identify the problem right away. Other disorders such as depression, obsessive-compulsive disorder, and social anxiety affect family members as well, but in a different way and perhaps not to the same extent. Furthermore, they are often not as embarrassing to the family as hoarding. Hoarding seems to point to some personal characteristic in the sufferer and the family members, when it truly does not. It is important that you see hoarding as a disorder, not some horrible personality characteristic of your parent.

WHEN YOU TELL OTHERS, WHAT DO YOU SAY?

First, think of what you want to convey to others. What has your personal secret been? Your secret could just be that your parent is a hoarder. Or it could be that you are frightened for your parent's safety and health. It could be something revealing about your past, such as how isolated you felt as a child; how embarrassed you were about the clutter; how your parent never even threw out garbage; how you did not do well in school and blame your parent today for your fate in life because you had nowhere to study or sleep; or how your parents always argued about the clutter and how you blamed yourself for not picking up after your mother when your father finally walked out. Now go back to the pros you listed to remind yourself why you want to share details of your situation with a particular person. What you convey may depend on whom you are conveying this family secret to. Let us look at some of the closest people in your life and then look at how you might convey it.

Your Children

Your children (if you have children) are, after you, the most important of the people who are likely to be affected by your parent's hoarding. They may not know exactly what is going on, but they probably know that something is not "right" with Grandma or Grandpa. Depending on the ages of your children, their ability to understand the situation will vary. If they are under the age of six, they probably will not have noticed anything unusual yet. If they are older, depending on their maturity, they may start to wonder why they never go to their grandparent's house. Perhaps you have made excuses, such as "Grandma is remodeling," "Grandpa is very busy," "Grandma is too old to have company," or "Grandpa never was too great with children in the house." On the other hand, maybe you are dealing with your own pain and rejection, and you say things like "Don't worry, she wasn't such a great mother either. Believe me, I had my share of issues with her. You wouldn't want to visit if you saw what her house looks like. It's a disaster zone; we couldn't walk inside." Or, perhaps you choose to be gently but firmly straightforward with your children, acknowledging your parent's position and your own: "I wish we could go over to Grandma's and Grandpa's, but Grandpa has a problem with clutter. He doesn't mean to keep everything, but he cannot throw things out. He wants to organize and have us over, but he just can't. I felt very frustrated living in the house with Grandpa, and though he always promised he'd change, I haven't seen it. But remember, we can always have Grandma and Grandpa come visit our house."

As you can see, depending on your feelings and thoughts about your parent's hoarding, you will convey the problem to your children accordingly. It is important, however, that you come to terms with your own feelings, as we discussed in chapters 4 and 5, before you speak to your children, as the goal of talking to them is to explain some of the behaviors surrounding the hoarding as fairly and honestly as you can.

Your Romantic Partner

If you have been dating someone for a while and things are starting to get serious, at some point you will probably want your romantic partner to meet your parents. Although this might not present a problem at first—for example, you may have dinner with your parents at a restaurant or, if you live on your own, you may invite them to your home—you might wonder how long you can play "Let's Avoid the House." The truth about your parent's hoarding will have to come out eventually, especially as your romantic partner becomes more a part of your life. Yet you are likely to hold back this information—worried perhaps that your partner will judge you, think badly of your parent, make fun of you or your parent, tell other people, or conclude that you must have the same hoarding tendencies or will become a hoarder too. You may rationalize keeping your parent's hoarding a secret in dozens of ways, such as:

It just isn't worth the trouble.

I won't let my mother's problem interfere with my love life.

If he loves me, he won't care.

What does my father's problem have to do with me?

Everyone has issues.

Her mother is not perfect either; she has no right to judge my family.

Yet, as you may have realized, sooner or later keeping such details to yourself will stand in the way of feelings of closeness and intimacy, in addition to taking a toll on your health. When you finally decide to tell your partner, keep in mind that you are not trying to defend or attack your parent. You are trying to explain a disorder that has affected your parent. Hoarding is not a reflection of a character defect, or a sign of dirtiness, but a disorder. Almost everyone is familiar with obsessive-compulsive disorder (OCD); and, as mentioned in chapter 1, hoarding falls within the OCD spectrum. Pointing out the similarity or relation of hoarding behavior to OCD may help your partner grasp the issue.

You might start off by saying that you want to share a private matter concerning your parent that you share only with very special people, people who might be affected by it. You might describe the problem in the following terms: "My father has a problem with hoarding. He has difficulty throwing things out, so whatever comes into the house stays in the house. I have lived with clutter all my life. My father is ashamed of this, although he can't help himself. It's a disorder, called hoarding." Appeal to your partner's sense of understanding, affirm your parent's good qualities, and share any relevant boundaries or compromises you have agreed on in your relationship with your parent. For example: "Please don't judge him because of his behavior. If it weren't for the state of the house, you'd never know he had this problem. As a person, he's no different from anybody else. However—and I'm sorry about this—in order to respect his wishes and his privacy, we won't be able to visit my parents' house."

Pick and choose whatever sorts of statements like these you feel comfortable making. When you explain the problem, do not attack your parent, as we have mentioned. But do not defend him or her, either. Feel free to discuss how his or her hoarding behavior affected you growing up, and still affects you today. Acknowledge both the disorder and its impact on you.

Your partner may ask questions. Be prepared to give answers that will help your partner understand as much as he or she needs to know about your particular situation. Common questions are "What is hoarding? What do you mean, he never throws anything out? What does the house look like? How does she have room to bring more and more stuff into the house?" You may be wondering whether or not you should give your partner specifics about the state of the home. Maybe it is best to ease your partner into the world of hoarding. In recent years, documentary TV programs such as TLC's Hoarding: Buried Alive and A&E's Hoarders have brought hoarding more to light; but, if your partner has seen these shows, he or she may also have some misconceptions about your parent's situation. Not every hoarding situation is as bad as those depicted on TV. Be sure to explain in your own way how the situation is for you and your family.

Your Parent's Neighbors

We have all come across neighbors who are nosy. Maybe your parent's neighbors suspect that something unusual is going on. Maybe they notice that there is no garbage going out or that there is an unusual smell coming from the home. Maybe they have an infestation and suspect that your parent's house is the source or cause of it. Maybe they can see that your parent's yard is cluttered. Maybe they see your parent going through other people's trash for recyclables. For any or all of these reasons, they may be concerned for people's health and safety; they may wonder whether something suspicious is going on; or they may worry that homes in the neighborhood will decrease in value if the problem is not addressed. So perhaps one day, or the next time they see you, the neighbors ask you whether all is well in the house. Or if the mess is noticeable, maybe the neighbors kindly ask you to have your parent clean it up. What do you say?

You could tell them to mind their own business, but that would probably not be very helpful and might escalate the tension. Again, avoid the temptation to defend or attack your parent. Try to be understanding of both sides of the situation and seek a solution. You may want to say something like "I'm sorry you are having difficulty with [the smell, the infestation, the mess, etc.]. I'll mention it to my parents and see whether there is anything they can do to help out." Be empathetic and solution oriented. It's true that a report by a neighbor can be a good thing for children of hoarders who have struggled for years with the conditions the neighbors are talking about, but it can also have devastating consequences for the parent, as some hoarders react so profoundly to the terror that complaints can elicit that they respond with suicidal ideation and attempts at self-harm. Therefore, it is best to take measures against this. Getting your parent to cooperate is one. You can explain that not doing so may mean eviction, condemnation of the house, the authorities sending people to the house, possibly an inspection by a judge, and most likely the housing authorities sending a crew to clean up the house.

So where can you start to take action? Perhaps you and your parent can hire an exterminator to eliminate pests (as much as possible), make space to have someone possibly enter a part of the house to remove mold, or organize the clutter outside of the home. You may be thinking right now that if these things were possible, then you would have done them already: *If I could have, then I would have.* It is probably true that you have been trying for a long time to get your parent to organize and throw things out. It is also true that in this book we have been telling you that sometimes it is best to not try to fix your parent's hoarding and just try to accept having uncomfortable feelings about it while behaving according to your values. But when it comes to the possiblity of a report by a neighbor, the consequences need to be explained to your parent loud and clear. Explain the possible consequences, look for a reasonable solution, and then, if your parent opts to do nothing, resume accepting your unpleasant feelings. Remember, you do not have control over your parent's behavior. So although you can approach the situation in a helpful manner, try to accept the outcome even if it is not what you had hoped for.

SUMMARY

Disclosing details about yourself and your life has health and relationship benefits, and sharing details of your parent's hoarding can help offset the negative emotional and physical effects you may have noticed. You are entitled to share your problems with others; however, remember that this is your parent's problem too. Think about your values, and base your decision about what to say to whom based on those values. It is important to think about the pros and cons of disclosing information about your parent's life and how it has affected you. There is a balance between being open and honest and protecting the privacy of your parent. Think about the significant people in your life, and share your feelings with them in an appropriate manner.

CHAPTER 8

If You Live with Your Parent

My life is at a complete standstill. When my daughter was born, I could not afford to continue paying rent on my own, so I had no choice but to move back in with my mother, knowing full well what I was signing on for. The house is as bad as or worse than I remembered. Bags and bags of stuff are all over the living room and piled to the ceiling in the hallways. All the rooms are navigable by only narrow, treacherous paths. It is a total nightmare. Thankfully, my mom cleared a space in one of the rooms for the baby and me to sleep and reside in, but time spent in any other part of the house is overwhelming, dangerous, and laborious. I can bathe the baby in the bathroom sink, which is accessible, but the shower is just storage now, so I have to shower at a friend's house. The refrigerator is broken and unreachable, so I purchased a small refrigerator to store my daughter's bottles, but I cannot store any of my own food. The rest of the kitchen is completely full of clutter, and I can't even prepare food, so I guess it's not a problem that I cannot store it. This arrangement cannot remain. I cannot put roots down in this environment, nor would that be fair to my daughter, but I cannot afford to live on my own. I am desperate and I feel completely backed into an incredibly cluttered corner.

—Jennifer

I f you, like Jennifer, are living with your parent who hoards, there is no doubt that not only does it affect you emotionally, but also it inconveniences you immensely every day. In this chapter, we aim to help you improve your quality of life, as well as to help you identify whether you will stay or leave, and, if you will leave, how to make a plan. You have a right to live without the clutter, and this chapter will help you explore what has stood in the way of that for you, as well as teach you strategies that will help you turn your life around.

REVISITING YOUR VALUES

In chapter 4, we asked you to complete a values-clarification exercise. This exercise asked you to examine the areas of life that you really value, as well as how successfully you have been living according to what is important to you. In chapter 6, we asked you to examine whether or not you are living in accordance with the importance that you place on your relationship with your parent. In this chapter, we will ask you to refer back to the values-clarification exercise yet again. What do you want your life to stand for, other than your relationship with your parent and the hoarding conditions?

Exercise: What Interferes with Committed Action?

List your valued life areas in order of importance. There is space for you to do this below. We would like you to then examine what interferes with value-oriented living and what prevents you from pursuing your values (i.e., taking committed action). If there is a discrepancy between your "Importance" and "Success" ratings in a valued area (see your responses to the values-clarification exercise in chapter 4), you can likely point to something that is getting in the way of acting on your values. List the obstacles to living in accordance with your values in this area.

1. Valued life area: _____

   Obstacles: _____

2. Valued life area: _____

   Obstacles: _____

3. Valued life area: _____

   Obstacles: _____

4. Valued life area: _____

   Obstacles: _____

5. Valued life area: _____

   Obstacles: _____

6. Valued life area: _____

   Obstacles: _____

7. Valued life area: _____

   Obstacles: _____

8. Valued life area: _____

   Obstacles: _____

9. Valued life area: _____

   Obstacles: _____

10. Valued life area: _____

Obstacles: _____

   As you complete this exercise, you will likely notice that certain obstacles relate to living in a home full of clutter. Maybe you are ashamed to bring dates to your house, so you have avoided really getting close to anyone romantically. Maybe the disorganization all around you has caused you in turn to be disorganized in a way that has interfered with your academic or professional accomplishment, as your work or study materials get scattered and lost among the mess.

   Be honest with yourself when completing this exercise. It may be tempting to say that *all* of your failed pursuits are the result of your living arrangement, but this is not an opportunity to *blame* your environment or your parent for your difficulties. Rather, we are asking you to take an honest look at what is missing from your life and what may be standing in the way of living the richest life that you can.

Acceptance and commitment therapy (ACT) offers this wisdom: we must practice accepting those unpleasant things in life that cannot be changed, but where important environmental changes can be made, it is important to make them in spite of any emotional repercussions.

Think of what your life *could be* like if you were free of the burden of living in a cluttered environment. You have likely known for a long time that the conditions in the home have stood in the way of acting on your values, and you have probably come to the conclusion on many occasions that you need to get out of there. But most likely, the clutter is not your only obstacle. What else is standing in the way of your living independently? Do you have financial concerns? Are you concerned about the effect that leaving your parent might have on your parent's welfare? With each reason that your mind comes up with, further ask yourself, *Why?* Why are you not financially capable of independent living? Why, specifically, are you concerned about your parent's welfare?

147

When you consider these questions, do any emotions emerge that you would like to avoid? You may fear that moving out would mean leaving your parent to loneliness, isolation, and dangerous or deplorable living conditions. You may have loads of reasons for why you *cannot* leave your parent or live on your own. Is it possible that maybe, in fact, you *can* work toward leaving, but the emotional expense of doing so is too much to bear? Maybe the image of your parent all alone breaks your heart; maybe you imagine your parent falling and sustaining a serious injury—an injury that may have been avoided, had you been there to prevent it. Maybe you imagine receiving the news that your parent has died, possibly due to injuries or long-standing health issues related to the conditions of the home, and you imagine the feeling of regret and guilt that you might experience.

Consider the extent to which these emotions might be influencing your decision to not move out of the home you share with your parent. Ask yourself, *When will I be free?* If things stay as they are, the progress of your life is completely contingent on your parent's decision to "turn over a new leaf," which is something that you have likely been waiting for, fruitlessly, for years. Is it fair for you to put your life on hold while you wait for your parent to choose a different path? And, more important, is the cost of letting things continue as they are (with you missing out on opportunities to pursue what is important to you) worth the benefit of what is being preserved (your parent's continued hoarding and your current living arrangement)? If the answer is no, we invite you to ask yourself whether you are willing to stay in the house. Do not be in a rush to say that you are not. It takes time to get used to the idea of a big change; do not expect to find moving out easy to embrace simply because you intellectually understand that it is something that you want. ACT theorists frequently refer to the Zen proverb "You cannot cross a chasm in two small jumps" to help illustrate the difficulty here (Hayes, Strosahl, and Wilson 1999, 241). You can sign on for a big challenge, or you can sign on for a minor challenge, but whatever the challenge, make sure you do it decisively and wholeheartedly.

We want to stress the importance of decisiveness (i.e., committed action) when choosing the life that you want for yourself, which we will explore in greater detail in the following section. At this point, if for one reason or another you do not believe that you can take steps toward leaving the home you share with your parent, we will generate a couple of more moderate challenges for you to undertake. And, as you begin to feel empowered by imposing boundaries in various areas of your life, true independence from your parent's hoarding will start to feel more and more within your grasp.

COMMITTED ACTION: BEHAVIORAL CONTRACTING

Regardless of whether independent living is currently a goal for you, behavioral contracting and committed action can help you establish boundaries, such as establishing private space within the home or maintaining functional communal areas. Committed action may also enable you to lead a life no longer dominated by the state of the home you share with your parent. As we introduced in chapter 4, committed action involves setting goals according to your values and carrying out actions toward those goals despite whatever obstacles may arise. In order to carry out committed action while residing in your parent's house, you should employ behavioral contracting. Boundaries, which we introduced the importance of setting and sticking to in chapter 3, are crucial to the development of a behavioral contract.

Exercise: Generate a Behavioral Contract and Use Committed Action

In this exercise, we will revisit how to create a behavioral contract (introduced in chapter 6). Afterward, we will discuss the use of committed action to help you stick to boundaries and enforce the contract.

Referring to the quote with which we opened this chapter, Jennifer valued healthy eating, but her mother's kitchen was dominated by clutter, which made cooking impossible. For Jennifer, committed action might involve establishing boundaries concerning the accumulation of items in the kitchen. Three concrete requests that Jennifer might make of her mother are as follows:

1. Safe access to the stove and stovetop

2. A clear counter space (at least two feet wide) for food preparation

3. Safe access to a working refrigerator

In exchange, Jennifer's mother might have some requests as well:

1. Jennifer will refrain from making critical comments about conditions of the home that are unrelated to her requests in the contract.

2. Jennifer will refrain from moving, discarding, or tampering with items in the home without my involvement or consent.

3. Jennifer will refrain from passive-aggressive or aggressive communication when discussing the hoarding situation.

With this example in mind, identify a valued area of your life that has been affected by your parent's hoarding. It may help to refer to your responses to the previous exercise. Based on this value, list three concrete goals that you would like your parent to comply with:

1.

2.

3.

Involve your parent in a discussion, using the communication strategies discussed in chapter 3. Explain the rationale for establishing a behavioral contract, and emphasize that this is an opportunity for both of you to work proactively toward mutually beneficial goals. This is not all about *your* frustrations—it is also about enabling your parent to identify areas of unhappiness. You may be surprised to find that your parent also has reasonable, concrete requests that you will be able to accommodate in exchange for your parent's accommodation of your reasonable requests. The following illustrates how you might successfully begin such a conversation.

Jennifer: Mom, I know that we are both unhappy with the current situation. I know that you feel that you have earned the right to live the way that you want to and that you resent my judgment about your home. Sometimes it is hard for me to keep my thoughts to myself, and I know that I need to work on this. I think that we both have things to work on in order to make things around here more pleasant for both of us. I want you to know that I do appreciate what you are doing for me: allowing me to live with you while I get back on my feet. In order to make this as happy a home as possible, I thought that maybe we could each come up with some requests for each other in order to improve our relationship and better enjoy each other. At this point, I really

151

don't want to force you to change everything about your lifestyle; I just want to be able to do some very basic things in your home while I am here. It is very important for me to be able to cook and bathe. I think you can understand why I feel this way. I am sure that you would like me to agree to certain things, as well. What do you say? Can we find a way to come to a compromise?

Reaching a compromise with your parent is just the beginning, because it is likely that at some point both you and your parent will fall short of meeting your respective ends of the bargain. It may be a good idea to schedule frequent "family meetings" at regular times, for the purpose of discussing how well both of you are keeping to the terms of the contract. If you are frustrated with your parent's lack of compliance with the contract, do not lose sight of your responsibilities. Just because your parent has breached the agreement does not mean that the contract was a failure or that you should give up. Any time you notice that your parent's behavior is in violation of your agreement, you will probably become very angry. Wait for your intense emotions to abate before discussing the violation with your parent. It is important that you keep the conversation productive; review the communication strategies that we elaborated in chapter 3, specifically those relating to assertive communication and validation. Using assertive language ("I" statements), with attention to validating your parent's feelings, will help you ride out difficult conversations, and hopefully keep the behavioral contract on track. Use these meetings to talk about both successes and failures in terms of the arrangement. Be willing to receive constructive criticism; it is important that your parent see you as willing to bend, so be flexible, with a calm disposition, when discussing the contract.

Whether the arrangement whereby you and your parent share a roof is temporary, long-term, or indefinite, committed action will enable you to better endure this period in your life. So take calm and measured steps, and try to let your values call the shots in terms of how you communicate with and what you request of your parent.

COMMITTED ACTION: MOVING OUT

If you live with your parent, moving out is the ultimate act of independence. Yet as we mentioned, many things might stand in the way of living on your own: financial concerns, concern for your parent's welfare, or codependency, to name a few.

Exercise: Identify Obstacles to Moving Out

In a notebook or on a separate piece of paper, list the considerations that are standing in the way of independent living for you, in order of how much they are interfering with your pursuit of independent living. List the most difficult item as number 1.

With each item, starting with the first (the most difficult item), examine the steps that would be necessary in order to unblock yourself from taking committed action. Answer the following questions:

1. When did this first become a problem?

2. What, realistically, would need to happen in order to solve the problem?

3. What steps would you need to follow to accomplish the goal you just described?

4. What obstacles stand in the way of each of these steps?

Let us use the example of Jennifer again. Jennifer might come up with the following answers about her problem of not having enough money:

1. When did this first become a problem? *When I gave birth to my daughter and was not able to afford to pay for both rent and child care.*

2. What, realistically, would need to happen in order to solve the problem? *I would need to make more money or find a cheaper child-care solution, while not sacrificing the quality of care.*

3. What steps would you need to follow to accomplish the goal you just described? *I would need to find a better-paying job, or I would have to appeal to friends and family members to help with child care.*

4. What obstacles stand in the way of each of these steps? *I have only a few college credits toward a degree in business. I am underqualified for most positions that would pay adequately. And my friends and family members all have their own responsibilities and their own priorities. It is difficult to find volunteers.*

As you can see, the process of distilling a solution involves stating the goal and carefully outlining the obstacles that stand in the way of accomplishing it, then examining what you must do to overcome these obstacles, as well as what further obstacles may follow. Though the four questions above will begin this process, it likely will not end there. Continue to further distill the problem, as well as the solution to the problem, by asking yourself *And what would be needed to fix that?* following each obstacle that your mind presents. While some solutions will remain unknown, you may come up with something that you had not thought of before. Explore this question with a close, supportive friend. Bring the exercise to your therapist or life coach. The goal here is adopting a problem-solving orientation. Most likely, there is a solution to your problem out there somewhere. It may not be easy or obvious; it may not be pleasant to pursue it; but the likelihood is that there is a solution. As you can see in Jennifer's example in the exercise above, no easy, clear-cut answers were generated from these questions alone. But, if Jennifer continues to ask herself "And what would be needed to fix that?" she may discover that it is necessary that she finish college, for example. And then, if she asks herself "What would be needed to fix *that*?" she may see that time and money are both further obstacles. Taking out student loans and attending night classes may not be ideal or easy, but they are solutions.

At the heart of this lies committed action. The value-oriented path is clearly not the easiest path, and with it inevitably comes more self-sacrifice. But it is the richest path—the one that will lead you in the direction of the most satisfying life.

SUMMARY

In this chapter, we explored how living in a home full of clutter stands in contrast to your ideal lifestyle. We examined how you might be able to turn things around and begin taking steps toward committed action, or value-oriented living. We identified two broad possible goals: behavioral contracting with your parent in order to make life under the same roof more functional and/or peaceful, and pursuit of independent living. We asked you to refer back to chapter 3 to practice assertive communication and use of validation in order to facilitate behavioral contracting. We also asked you to examine what might be standing in the way of your pursuit of independent living. If you have been at an impasse in the pursuit of independent living, committed action may be the solution.

CHAPTER 9

Potential Adversaries and Allies in the Community

Whether your parent lives in an apartment, a single-family home, or an assisted-living facility, your parent's hoarding can interfere with the lives of others, as well as create safety and health hazards. If and when the hoarding gets to a point where it is no longer manageable, concerned individuals may notify various local authorities, who may then intervene. Thus you may one day find yourself trying to help your parent deal with actions and measures taken by government agencies and others aimed at controlling the mess. For this reason, it is important to learn about the various figures and agencies that may get involved. Often you will find that you can work with them toward mutually beneficial goals—in other words, you can turn these adversaries into allies.

Perhaps you yourself have notified an authority figure or sought the involvement of a government agency in your parent's hoarding, out of sheer frustration with the situation. Or perhaps one day you will. Even if you are the one who appeals to the authorities to do something about the problem, their involvement will undoubtedly put strain on you and your parent who must deal with them. Therefore, you should know as much as possible about whom you are dealing with and what they can and cannot do.

NEIGHBORS

Neighbors, as we discussed in chapter 7, are likely to have at least an inkling that something is amiss in the home of your parent who hoards. They may complain about the appearance of the home or yard and call the town or city hall and ask for guidance; or they may make a report to the police or fire department. Often the police department will not intervene if there has been no outright disturbance, such as a fight. On the other hand, the fire department may come and look around the house for any indication of a fire hazard. Normally, they would not be able to enter the house without permission when doing such an inspection. However, neighbors who call the town or city hall will often be directed to the housing department of the county where your parent resides; once the housing department gets involved, it can authorize fire department personnel, judges (see below), and others to enter a dwelling.

However, neighbors can be turned into allies when and if your parent is able to allow some cleanup efforts. Our experience has been that if you tell the neighbors that you are going to be leaving a trash receptacle or portable storage unit in the driveway as you work on cleaning up the house, they will be happy to hear it. They will be on your side and supportive.

If your parent will agree only to smaller-scale cleanup efforts, or if you are having trouble getting your parent to do anything about the problem at all, consider talking to the neighbors one by one. If you do this, make sure to let your parent know in advance so that it does not come as a surprise to learn what you have told the neighbors. Tell them that your parent is embarrassed about the conditions they have probably noticed (e.g., accumulation of items, unkempt lawn, or disrepair—there is no need to divulge too much) and certainly does not want to maintain these conditions, but has a true problem. Assure them that you are aware of the problem and you are working on it. Vouch that your parent does not mean any harm, and convince them how much your parent wants to live in the neighborhood for years to come. Try to get them to feel compassion for how embarrassed your parent is, and they may go from complaining to offering to help. When you explain the situation and get them to view the problem as part of a disorder and one that your parent wants to straighten out, this allows them to ally themselves with you.

LANDLORDS

If your parent is a renter, at first your parent's landlord may politely ask your parent to clear out the clutter, but sooner or later your parent may face eviction if he or she does not comply. Most likely there will be many warning notices before your parent receives an eviction notice, and it is always better to try to intervene before the situation reaches that point. Perhaps you can step in and speak to a housing manager or apartment manager before the landlord gets involved. However, once an eviction notice has been served, it is best to consult with an eviction defense attorney or a volunteer legal representative.

An eviction defense attorney will look to see whether the case is what is called an "unlawful detainer case." The attorney will try to find out whether your parent has a disability that would require reasonable accommodation to be made prior to eviction.

It may be important to prove that your parent has a disability in the form of a psychological disorder, because unless there is a problem (such as a disorder) that can be treated or remedied, the fact that the hoarding conditions have created a "nuisance" may be sufficient legal grounds for eviction. A nuisance, in legal terminology, is a serious threat to one's health and safety and/or a fire-code violation. In other words, if your parent's hoarding behavior is deemed to be untreatable, then the determination of a "nuisance" means the court will not show any leniency.

It may also be helpful to have a report from a mental health or other professional that shows that your parent who hoards has a diagnosable medical or mental health condition. If you do not have such a report, perhaps you can convince your parent to seek treatment or at least a consult, with the promise that a diagnosis will be helpful to ward off the authorities for a while. This report hopefully will demonstrate to a court that the nuisance is caused by a disorder fitting a diagnostic category known as hoarding, and that this disorder is treatable.

If it can be demonstrated to the court that your parent has a recognizable disorder, the landlord must show that accommodation was granted in the form of time to clear the clutter or seek treatment by a cognitive behavioral therapist or psychiatrist. If accommodation was not granted, your parent can file suit against the property owner for violation of the Fair Housing Act, which prohibits discrimination against those with disabilities (you may read the full text of this law at www.justice.gov/crt/about/hce/title8.php).

HOUSING-COURT JUDGES

Housing-court judges hear cases in which there is an eviction notice. They determine whether there is a "nuisance" and how to deal with it. A housing-court judge does not have the authority to mandate a cleanup or require your parent to seek treatment, but can grant time extensions for these purposes. The judge can also require that your parent be moved to another apartment rather than evicted outright, if your parent lives in an apartment.

If the housing-court judge believes that your parent is unable to adequately represent himself or herself, the court will appoint a guardian *ad litem* ("for the suit") to assist your parent. Often the local adult protective services (APS) agency will become involved. APS can orchestrate a cleanup, but only on consent of your parent (or your parent's guardian). The judge may make a personal visit to your parent's home to make a determination of a nuisance. Most often, housing-court judges deal with apartment dwellings, but sometimes single-family home cases come before them. In severe cases of hoarding in which there are health-code, safety-code, and fire-code violations that cause the judge to perceive the home as a danger to the well-being of those living in it or "unlivable," the judge may condemn the house. Condemnation of a hoarder's house occurs only after the hoarder has been given ample time to remedy the situation and does not do so within a specified amount of time. If the judge condemns your parent's home, then the court must find a placement for your parent, and the county has to pay for the repairs and renovations. Although housing-court judges try to avoid condemnations, they may not always be able to.

CHILD PROTECTIVE SERVICES

When children under the age of eighteen are living in a cluttered environment that may be deemed unsafe or unhealthy, child protective services (CPS) may become involved. Although teachers, school personnel, physicians, and mental-health professionals are mandated to report any form of child abuse or neglect—and that includes a home full of clutter—anyone can make a call to CPS anonymously. When CPS gets involved, the agency sends a worker to evaluate whether children are able to move about freely in the house, have a bed to sleep in, are fed adequately, and are safe from dangers such as high accident risk and poor air quality (e.g., due to molds and mildew). CPS also looks to make sure that children are provided with everything they need for normal neurological development, such as room to play with objects that enhance visual-motor coordination, spatial relations, and so on.

You should know that CPS generally does not want to remove children from a home unless absolutely necessary. If CPS workers feel compelled to remove a child, they usually place the child with a relative until the situation is resolved. That is, they return the child to the home immediately after safety and health concerns have been satisfactorily addressed.

Perhaps you have moved out but have younger siblings who still live with your parent who hoards. Relatives can help children when there is hoarding in the house by spending time out of the house with them—inviting them for sleepovers, hosting birthday parties, taking them out for various events, and so forth. It is important to show children that they have options outside of the house. Do not forget that young children of hoarders are often isolated. They are not able to invite people over to their house, and therefore their social life is often limited. Also, they fear the hoarding being discovered, and therefore they would rather go unnoticed.

Sometimes a hoarder's spouse or partner will call CPS anonymously just to get the authorities involved, in the hope that this will influence the hoarder to change. The tipster may be genuinely concerned for the well-being of the children, or may see calling CPS as the only way to get the hoarder into treatment (as CPS can mandate treatment). Sometimes hoarding is used as a reason for seeking custody of children. Again, CPS is not looking to take children away from their parents, but to arrange for a safe and healthy environment for them to grow up in.

ADULT PROTECTIVE SERVICES

Adult protective services (APS) serves those aged sixty-five and over who are dependent or have disabilities. APS provides the following services:

- Referral for psychiatric and/or medical examination and ongoing care

- Assistance in obtaining and recertifying Medicaid and home care

- Assistance in obtaining public assistance benefits and obtaining and recertifying Supplemental Security Income (SSI) or Social Security Disability (SSD) benefits

- Assistance in making applications for payment of rental and utility arrears

- Petitioning the housing court for a guardian *ad litem* to assist with eviction prevention

- Identification of alternative living arrangements

- Management of Social Security benefits

- Referrals to the police department and district attorney to address allegations of exploitation and abuse

- Heavy-duty cleaning services

- Petitioning the state supreme court to assign a guardian to manage one's financial and domestic affairs

You or another family member, your parent's neighbors, fire department personnel, police officers, lawyers, housing-court judges, or representatives of other governmental agencies may notify APS of your parent's hoarding. Once APS is involved, you should see the APS workers as your allies, even if you did not wish for this to happen. They are there to help you find a positive solution to safety-code, health-code, and fire-code violations caused by hoarding conditions. Helping people find reasonable solutions to problems to keep them from being evicted is part of what they are trained to do.

If your parent is suspected of not being able to care for himself or herself, APS may ask you or another relative to act as your parent's guardian (called a "conservator," in some states). A guardian's role is to provide for a person's basic needs such as food, clothing, shelter, and medical treatment; oversee the person's estate; and manage the person's money and assets. If you are considering becoming your parent's guardian, be sure to consult with an elder law attorney so that you fully understand the legal obligations of being a guardian. If no one wants to assume the role of guardian, APS may appoint an attorney or other professional to the role.

APS may try to work with your parent either to avoid an eviction or to ensure that your parent is safe in the home. APS workers will go into the home and try to get it cleaned out enough for it to be in a reasonable living condition. Although they do not have the resources to approach the problem from a therapeutic perspective, they may make a recommendation that your parent seek treatment for hoarding. APS may request a cleanup, or, as it is sometimes called, a "clean out."

THE FIRE DEPARTMENT

The fire department may get involved when there are fire-code violations such as the following:

- Blocked entrances or exits

- Nonfunctioning smoke alarms

- Appliances that are covered with fire-hazard items

- Exposed or jury-rigged electrical wiring

- Items that are too close to the boiler or heating system

- Combustible items that are placed where they should not be

- Burning of dangerous items in the fireplace

If the above conditions exist in your parent's house, the house is considered a fire hazard and thus the fire department has the authority to intervene, for the safety of its inhabitants as well as the community. Clutter can turn a minor fire into a major one that would affect not only your parent's home but neighboring ones as well.

Fire-department personnel must by law investigate any and all fire-code violations. Sometimes firefighters may come to a hoarder's house for a minor fire, or some other reason, only to find the condition of the house to be a fire hazard (see chapter 2). They may notice an abundance of combustible goods, or they may note possible electrical problems. They may try to work with the hoarder, giving him or her time to address the problems, but they can also request that the housing court get involved and possibly condemn the residence.

THE POLICE DEPARTMENT

Although the police usually do not get involved in cases of hoarding, neighbors may call the police when they witness what appears to be suspicious activity. For example, sometimes hoarders who are adamant about recycling try to recycle their neighbors' goods as well; a neighbor who sees your parent roaming the neighborhood looking into other people's trash cans may call the police. Someone who is uncomfortable with the way your parent walks around looking for items that seem free for the taking may also call the police. A few hoarders have resorted to stealing when they felt as if they "must have" an item; this may obviously lead to police involvement.

AN ANIMAL HUMANE SOCIETY

If your parent is an animal hoarder, what started out as a mission of mercy may turn into a completely chaotic situation. It may reach the point where there are so many animals that your parent simply cannot provide proper care for them all. They may not have enough food, and they may even attack one another; some of them may be in need of veterinary care. There may even be dead animals among the hoard. Because these conditions constitute animal abuse, your local animal humane society may be able to help. Sometimes an animal humane society is able to send someone to the premises to provide care for neglected animals. You may want to visit the website of the Humane Society of the United States (www.humane society.org). You can also check with the American Society for the Prevention of Cruelty to Animals (ASPCA) (aspca.org).

SUMMARY

There are many agencies that are invested in helping members of the community such as your parent. Those who appear to be adversaries can be turned into allies. Explaining that your parent has an accepted diagnosable condition will enable people to work with you. However, it is also important for your parent to understand that any condition in the home that is deemed to be unsafe, unhealthy, or a fire-code violation by the housing court and/or adult protective services (APS) can lead to an eviction or to condemnation of the house. Govenment agencies take hoarding very seriously. Knowing what service each agency provides will allow you to better help your parent. Perhaps sharing what you have learned in this chapter will enable your parent to understand better the potential consequences of the problem, before it becomes necessary to use what you have learned.

CHAPTER 10

Inheriting the Mess

HOW TO TACKLE CLEANING UP WHEN MOURNING THE LOSS OF YOUR PARENT

Your long history with your parent who hoards is probably the source of both many bitter and many sweet memories for you. The likelihood is that your parent has had a significant hand in shaping who you are, and when your parent passes, it will be an emotionally difficult time, to say the least.

The death of a parent is a tragic event for anyone. As the child of a hoarder, you may have the added difficulty of dealing with an estate full of clutter. For some, it will be necessary to decline this task. Others will want to take an active role in resolving matters of the estate. It is likely that you will have some kind of deadline for sifting through the clutter and preparing your parent's home for functional use again, whether you or someone else will live in it.

It's possible that, from your earliest memory, nothing of substantial value has been visible to you among your parent's clutter. However, your parent likely has some valuable items, although they will be difficult to locate. Remember that oftentimes, hoarders store valuable objects in places where you would not necessarily expect to find them. In this chapter, assuming that your parent who hoards has recently passed, we will help you sift through the clutter in a reasonable way, in order to facilitate this process. We will also provide suggestions for coping with your parent's passing in a way that will allow you to honor your parent's memory, despite the bittersweet quality of many of your recollections.

THE DISCARDING PROCESS

Let us assume that unfortunately the responsibility to save the important items among your parent's possessions has fallen on you. And while you did not ask for this responsibility, it has now been dropped on your plate. This chapter will help you manage it properly.

When sifting through your parent's estate, you should expect to find three categories of things worth saving: sentimental objects, valuable objects, and useful objects. Ironically, sentimentality, value, and usefulness may have been your parent's reasons for saving these objects in the first place. Of course, your objective is to sort items in a more discriminative way than your parent was able to. Below, we will break down these reasons to save and provide criteria for discarding items that are not necessarily important, valuable, or useful. If you, like your parent, have hoarding tendencies, this process might be quite difficult. If you are at the other end of the spectrum and do not like to keep *anything*, this task might be equally difficult. Either way, keep in mind that the objective here is to preserve what should be preserved and to discard what should be discarded.

The First Step

The first step of the process involves discarding items that are obviously valueless. If your parent hoarded garbage, this is an easy place to start. Discarding items that are unquestionably useless will be the easiest part of this process. Such items might include disposable cups or other food and beverage containers; sources of obvious insect or rodent infestation; or old newspapers or magazines that your parent had no sentimental reason for saving. Depending on what type of hoarder your parent was, this task will make up more or less of your endeavor.

If your parent's house is particularly squalid, for this step you may need to hire professional junk or debris removers—it may be too hazardous for you to ender the house.

As you are discarding items that are understandably unpleasant to handle, be sure to take care of yourself. If you find yourself getting tired or excessively disgusted, be sure to schedule breaks. Do not attempt to complete this task in one day, one weekend, one week, or one month; in other words, think about the time frame loosely. Take your time, and pursue this endeavor little by little if you can. Solicit the help of friends and family. This is not your burden to bear alone. You have a right to seek help from others who are involved and others who care about you. Do not forget that this is a difficult time for you for many reasons, and it is important that you do not undertake the task of the cleanup alone.

Below, we will discuss discarding things that will require more attention. This can be both an emotional process and a challenging one from a decision-making perspective.

Sentimental Hoarding

If your parent was a sentimental hoarder, the likelihood is that you will be bombarded by an endless supply of artifacts from your life and your parent's life (e.g., all of your childhood toys; old photo albums; every outfit that you ever wore as a child; everything that your other parent owned, if your other parent passed first; or every last homework assignment that you completed). The task of winnowing down these items to only the most meaningful ones may seem very daunting. After all, where is the line between sentimentally necessary and unnecessary? Most likely, this is the same conundrum that your parent faced: not being able to distinguish where this threshold lay.

We would like you to begin by deciding how much space you would like to devote to sentimental items; or, if you are aiming to place items in storage, how many boxes of sentimental belongings you are looking to store. Once this volume or number has been determined, you have your threshold; the amount of material that can fit into the boxes puts a limit on what you can save. Hold yourself to this restriction; if you find yourself sparing too many objects, just remember that you will have to pare the items down, in order to fit them into the number of boxes that you decided.

It may be very difficult to discard items that held sentimental value to your parent. Many items among your parent's belongings may seem valuable or important, especially if you identify with your parent's hoarding behavior, to some extent. However, we will ask you to take an honest look at your priorities and your own values to help you make the distinction between what should be saved and what should not. If you find that you answer yes to several of the following questions when considering a certain object, then this object might be a candidate for the "save" category.

Does this item make me emotional?

Do I have any emotional attachment to this item?

Does this item allow me to experience some emotion that I would not otherwise be able to experience?

What is the likelihood that I will use this item and/or reflect on this item in my lifetime?

Realistically speaking, will this item become a family heirloom?

If I part with this item, will I miss it?

This process may take a long time, but if you are honest with yourself, keeping these questions in mind while sorting through your parent's belongings, you will be more likely to find the balance between what is best saved and what is best thrown away.

It is very important to take care of yourself throughout the cleaning process. Your mind and body may resist the task of processing your parent's possessions and, correspondingly, your feelings about your recent loss. You may frequently become tired, become distracted or feel "foggy" and disconnected, or become upset or sad. To minimize the toll that the cleaning process will undoubtedly take on you, follow the steps below in the interest of self-care.

1. Before each cleanup session, decide how much time you are aiming to spend, so that you don't try to get too much done in one day. Hold yourself to this time limit, more or less.

2. Assign yourself specific tasks. Break big or complicated tasks into chunks.

3. When you notice that you are having difficulty with some part of the cleanup, give yourself permission to take a break, or put the task aside for the day.

Hoarding Based on Worth

You may want to investigate the worth of certain of your parent's belongings before discarding them. While it is true that individuals who hoard often overestimate the value of their cluttered possessions, there may be something of value to salvage, whether you are looking to keep any of these items or looking to sell. And even though your parent's home may look like a junkyard, you would not want to miss the diamond in the rough.

Items that are commonly hoarded because they may be valuable include dolls, books, antique household items, antique items in general, machinery, jewelry, stuffed animals, and other keepsake collections. It is a good idea to have this collection appraised, especially if your parent was an enthusiast of something that you do not have an interest in or knowledge of. You also may get a sense of what your parent's collection is worth by exploring typical prices online, on shopping or auction sites. Although your parent probably overestimated its actual value, any collection is likely worth *something*.

Based on the outcome of your inquiries, you may choose to save, sell, or discard your parent's collection. If you feel some sentimental reason for keeping an aspect of it, be conservative in choosing what and how much to save. Choose one or a few *prized* elements of the collection, as a way of honoring your parent's interest in the collected items, and let the rest go, knowing that you do not want to demonstrate the same behavioral pattern of dysfunctional saving that caused so much suffering while your parent was alive.

If you are planning to sell items from a collection of your parent's, online auction sites can offer an enormous sample of interested buyers who can view photos of, bid on, and purchase your parent's items. Otherwise, antique shops, secondhand stores, pawn shops, or specialty shops may be interested in purchasing items from your parent's collection, provided that the items are in good enough condition.

If you have decided to discard your parent's collection, but find that you are struggling with the emotional implications of doing so, you may experience some thoughts associated with a hoarding mentality. You may have thoughts such as:

What if I regret throwing this away?

What would Mom think if she saw me discarding this?

I know that we had our difficulties, but I loved Dad. I will never see him again—can I really get rid of the things that meant so much to him?

While this collection was a source of so much conflict in life, can I really dishonor my mother's wishes as far as whether or not to keep these items after her death?

Despite the emotionally charged nature of these thoughts, do not let your mind get away with this kind of emotional coercion. This line of thinking may have been responsible for your parent's hoarding in the first place. The reason why discarding items (or rather, not discarding items) caused so much conflict between you and your parent is because hoarding behaviors are dysfunctional, insidious, and ultimately destructive. Do not fall victim to them yourself as you are choosing what to save among the items in your parent's collection. If you find that you want to save a few items to represent your parent's interests, this is fine; just set a limit based on intellectual reason, rather than emotional desperation. Remember that your relationship with and your love for your parent is not tangible; it is not contained in any object. If you find that you are struggling to make difficult decisions regarding what to discard, this is also fine; let the emotional experience pass, and pick the task up again tomorrow. It may be helpful to refer to some of the resources available to hoarders themselves, such as *Overcoming Compulsive Hoarding* by Fugen Neziroglu, Jerome Bubrick, and Jose Yaryura-Tobias (New Harbinger Publications, 2004).

Instrumental Hoarding

If your parent's possessions include items that your parent suspected would have use one day (as in instrumental hoarding), the same rules do not apply. It is not necessary to investigate the potential value of instrumental items, assuming that you do not have the tendency to hoard useful items as well. Rather, you can simply use common sense: expired foods and medications can be thrown away; old newspapers and mail can be discarded; book collections can be donated (assuming that the books are not clearly valuable). If your parent accumulated a collection of broken appliances or machinery, you may want to discard these items (assuming that they have no probable historical value). If your parent saved containers and other organizational tools, again, you may see a pretty clear dividing line between what to save and what to discard.

However, clearing a house full of items that were saved for their instrumental value also has its share of special considerations. Because hoarders tend to have difficulty organizing and discerning valuable objects from invaluable objects, it is more likely than not that your parent placed extremely valuable items (e.g., checks, cash, and jewelry) alongside objects of no value (e.g., junk mail, expired food, and old newspapers). Furthermore, due to the paranoia that often accompanies a hoarder's mentality, it is not unlikely that your parent was suspicious of financial institutions and therefore may have been storing cash in a variety of unusual places. You will need to judge whether the likely value of such items, objects, and cash will outweigh the time, effort, and emotional investment required for you to separate them from the rest of the items in the home. You may wish to revisit the Values Clarification exercise in chapter 4 to help you decide which actions are best in keeping with your values and goals.

COPING WITH BEREAVEMENT

As we mentioned above, the death of a parent is cause for anyone to mourn, but it is an especially conflicted time for the child of a hoarder. You are not a "bad person" if you feel a complex mix of deep loss, resentment, sadness, relief, and guilt for feeling relief, among many other emotional reactions. Anyone in your situation would feel pulled in many different directions emotionally. Do not make your suffering worse by labeling and criticizing your emotional response.

After all, your relationship with your parent was always complicated; why should that be any different in death than it was in life? The task on your plate is not to rewrite history, sugarcoat your relationship with your parent, or banish all bitter feelings that you have after your parent's death. Rather, you and your parent are owed an accurate picture of your parent's legacy. Below, we will introduce a few strategies for coping with the loss of your parent, given the emotional burden that you are experiencing.

Your Rights and Responsibilities in the Grieving Process

There is no right or wrong way to grieve, no prescribed length of time that you are supposed to grieve for, nor any rule that you even have to grieve. Emotional processing of loss is entirely individual, and your grieving process will be unique to you. Therefore, do not feel pressured to conform to any time line or behavioral response; grieve in a way that feels natural to you. For some, the process may not even feel like grief at all. You may think that you should be grieving, but feel relief and liberation instead, or a sense of apathy. The lack of grief may make you feel guilty or ashamed, as you compare how you "should" feel to how you actually do. Do not do this. Feelings are just feelings, neither right nor wrong, and you should be true to them.

If you choose to grieve, do not forget to take care of yourself. If you do not think about your own physical health, especially in the early stages of your bereavement, important self-care activities may fall by the wayside. You must be your first priority at this point. If during the grieving process, you feel depleted in terms of health, emotional strength, and energy, take these physical and emotional cues as an indication that you need to slow down and take care of your basic needs (sleeping, eating, and basic wellness activities, as well as your emotional needs) first.

If you are feeling considerable pain, it is best not to try to force the pain of your loss away: when difficult emotions are denied, they tend to come out in dysfunctional ways, such as substance abuse, depersonalization (feelings of detachment or unreality), anger, or aggression. Give yourself time to process your loss, and allow yourself the chance to feel weak and vulnerable as a result.

You do not have to do this alone. It is important that you lean on loved ones, friends, and mental-health professionals during this time. Consider joining a support group aimed at managing grief, if you have not done so already. Even though your loss cannot be "fixed" (i.e., your parent cannot be returned to you, and the frustrations of your relationship with your parent cannot be remedied), it is important to give a voice to your feelings repeatedly, as this will allow you to better process and come to terms with them. One exercise that we recommend in this process is the composition of a "reflection letter," as a way to initiate honest processing of your feelings about your parent and about your loss.

Exercise: Write a Reflection Letter

You may have already written a eulogy or an obituary for your parent. Now, we would like you to write something different: a letter to your parent.

Really, this letter is not for your parent, but for you. Writing in a notebook or on a separate piece of paper, feel free to be completely honest about how you are feeling, in terms of how devastated, hurt, and angry you are. Let this be a final summary of your relationship with your parent, including both positive and negative reflections. Write your thoughts and feelings as they flow, in "stream of consciousness" mode, even if the result is long and rambling. Do not spare harsh words for your parent if you have them; this activity is about you, and processing your loss, not about speaking assertively or nonjudgmentally. Your parent will not hear or read this. Describe your feelings about your history, how your parent's actions influenced you, what you learned from your parent, what you appreciate your parent for, and what you do not appreciate your parent for. Explore your complex and sometimes seemingly contradictory feelings. At some times in your letter you may express guilt, remorse, and regret; at other times you may express anger and resentment; still other aspects of your letter may elaborate on the wonderful aspects of your upbringing and the valuable character traits you inherited. What follows is an example of the beginning of a reflection letter.

Dear Mom,

Sometimes, like now, I miss you so much it is painful. It has been three months since your passing, and while things are starting to go back to normal, I feel like there is still so much that I want to say to you. Toward the end of your life, we did not have much of a relationship. This was a source of tremendous stress for me, as well as tremendous guilt. You forced us out, but I was relieved in a way to not have to witness your decline. I am ashamed of that thought now, but I am also so angry that you never seemed to want to try. To have a relationship with your family was not incentive enough to confront your hoarding problem. One by one, you alienated each of us, and it became clear that you had no intention of changing. We just wanted our mom in our lives, in our children's lives. It is heartbreaking to think that your grandkids never really had a relationship with you. I also think that I gave up on trying to compromise with you. I have many regrets about how the last five years have gone. I wish that I had invited you to Christmas that year. I wish that I had tried harder to keep the lines of communication open, because I will never have that time back. There was a lot about our relationship that was precious to me. When I was a kid, you tried to make everything fun. You would sew that rainbow patch that I loved onto every outfit that I wore throughout kindergarten. You helped me care for that injured bird that I found, even though you knew it was going to die. You taught me to respect nature and stay in the present moment. You taught me that kindness is one of the most important things that we can offer each other. I carry these lessons into my own parenting. And in these ways, your presence in my life has made all the difference. That said, I also feel damaged and ashamed because of the conditions that I was forced to grow up in...

It is likely that your feelings about your parent are similarly complex. Do not hesitate to be honest about what those feelings are; no one else ever needs to see this letter.

Your Parent's Memory

Many people who have experienced a difficult childhood find it hard to remember the people who impose the difficulty on them. Some live in pain for years to come. Others find solace in activism or in spreading awareness of a cause that was relevant to the person who died. Activism centered on hoarding and obsessive-compulsive spectrum disorders gives some children of hoarders a sense that they are helping others to understand the disorder and the impact of hoarding on families and communities. It may allow you, too, to feel as though your parent's struggles and your own struggles were not in vain. If you are interested, you might begin by looking for volunteer opportunities on the website of the International Obsessive Compulsive Disorder Foundation (ocfoundation.org), or join the organization Children of Hoarders (www.childrenofhoarders.com).

SUMMARY

In this chapter, we examined the different obstacles that you may encounter after your parent who hoarded has passed on. We examined special considerations for clearing out the clutter when your parent's hoarding problems related to instrumental hoarding, sentimental hoarding, and value-based hoarding. We offered suggestions for managing the cleanup process, with each of these hoarding subtypes in mind. We also provided suggestions for dealing with your feelings relating to the death of your parent, including the composition of a letter to your deceased parent, and ways to make sense of your experience as the child of a hoarder through work that could promote greater understanding of hoarding and help for those involved.

Resources

SUGGESTED WEBSITES

Children of Hoarders

www.childrenofhoarders.com

This comprehensive site offers detailed accounts of the experiences of children of hoarders, as well as online social support opportunities, including information about hoarding, cleaning considerations, and hoarding task forces in your area. The Children of Hoarders site also allows you to search for any in-person support groups for children of hoarders that might be meeting in your area.

Children of Hoarders and Spouses of Children of Hoarders Online Support Group

health.groups.yahoo.com/group/childrenofhoarders

This online support group, affiliated with Children of Hoarders, offers further opportunities for social support for adult children of hoarders and those related to them. It focuses on the effects of a parent's hoarding behavior on those children who have endured it.

Adult Children of Hoarders Facebook Page

www.facebook.com/groups/337932535768

This Facebook group allows adult children of hoarders to convene, seek support, and share their difficult experiences living as children of hoarders.

Friends/Family of Hoarders/Clutterers

health.groups.yahoo.com/group/Friends-FamilyofHoarders
-Clutterers

A support group for children, family members, and friends of compulsive hoarders, dedicated to providing its members with a venue to discuss hoarding behaviors in the family.

International Obsessive Compulsive Disorders Foundation

www.iocdf.org

This website offers information about obsessive compulsive disorders, as well as contact information for therapists in your area who practice evidence-based treatment for these disorders.

Association for Behavioral and Cognitive Therapies

www.abct.org

This site offers contact information for professionals trained in cognitive behavioral therapy (CBT) in your area, who may be able to help you and/or your parent who hoards. It also contains basic information about CBT to better help you understand the CBT treatment process.

Anxiety and Depression Association of America

www.ADAA.org

This organization provides comprehensive information about disorders on the anxiety spectrum, which obsessive compulsive disorder (OCD) and its subtypes were once on. Its website offers contact information for a network of providers practicing evidence-based treatment for anxiety disorders, which may be of use to children of hoarders and hoarders themselves.

Institute for Challenging Disorganization

www.challengingdisorganization.org

This organization uses the latest in education, research, and strategies around chronic disorganization to assist those who struggle with it. It also allows users to access a network of trained organization specialists. Visitors can also download the Clutter-Hoarding Scale in order to better understand their hoarding and/or cluttering behaviors, or those of a friend or family member.

Clutterers Anonymous

sites.google.com/site/clutterersanonymous/Home?pli=1

A 12-step support network for "clutterers," who often meet criteria for hoarding disorder, though they do not always demonstrate quite as intense an attachment to certain items as those diagnosed as hoarders do. Visitors to the website can access information about clutter, problematic cluttering, and resources for clutterers.

Messies Anonymous

www.messies.com

Messies Anonymous is a 12-step program for people who identify as "messies," and offers a range of support options for them, including in-person groups in your area.

Fly Lady

www.flylady.net

Founded by Marla Cilley, FLY Lady (whose acronym stands for Finally Loving Yourself) is a user-friendly website for clutterers and others who simply want practical, warm suggestions for getting the home, and one's life, back in order. The website offers many detailed tips for tackling both the problem of extreme clutter and day-to-day responsibilities involving the home. Participants are taught a "baby steps" approach to decluttering, making this website an excellent resource for those who have already undergone more intensive treatment for cluttering behaviors.

National Association of Professional Organizers

www.napo.net

This site offers visitors access to a network of expert organizers certified to contend with the task of cleaning up a home in which hoarding has occurred, with detailed descriptions of organizing services and the contact information for professionals licensed to provide them.

SUGGESTED READING

Neziroglu, Fugen, Jerome Bubrick, and Jose A. Yaryura-Tobias. 2004. *Overcoming Compulsive Hoarding: Why You Save and How You Can Stop*. Oakland, CA: New Harbinger Publications.

Tolin, David F., Randy O. Frost, and Gail Steketee. 2007. *Buried in Treasures: Help for Compulsive Acquiring, Saving, and Hoarding*. New York: Oxford University Press.

Tompkins, Michael A., and Tamara L. Hartl. 2009. *Digging Out: Helping Your Loved One Manage Clutter, Hoarding, and Compulsive Acquiring*. Oakland, CA: New Harbinger Publications.

Sholl, Jessie. 2010. *Dirty Secret: A Daughter Comes Clean about Her Mother's Compulsive Hoarding*. New York: Gallery Books.

Steketee, Gail, and Randy O. Frost. 2010. *Stuff: Compulsive Hoarding and the Meaning of Things*. New York: Houghton Mifflin Harcourt.

Paxton, Matt, and Phaedra Hise. 2011. *The Secret Lives of Hoarders: True Stories of Tackling Extreme Clutter*. New York: Penguin Group.

Zasio, Robin. 2011. *The Hoarder in You: How to Live a Happier, Healthier, Uncluttered Life*. New York: Rodale Books.

References

Baikie, K. A., and K. Wilhelm. 2005. "Emotional and Physical Health Benefits in Expressive Writing." *Advances in Psychiatric Treatment* 11 (5): 338–46.

Bellack, A. S., G. L. Haas, and A. M. Tierney. 1996. "A Strategy for Assessing Family Interaction Patterns in Schizophrenia." *Psychological Assessment* 8: 190–99.

Boye, B., H. Bentsen, I. Ulstein, T. H. Notland, A. Lersbryggen, O. Lingjærde, and U. F. Malt. 2001. "Relatives' Distress and Patients' Symptoms and Behaviors: A Prospective Study of Patients with Schizophrenia and Their Relatives." *Acta Psychiatrica Scandinavica* 104: 42–50.

Calvocoressi, L., C. Mazure, S. V. Kasl, J. Skolnick, D. Fisk, S. J. Vegso, B. L. Van Noppen, and L. H. Price. 1999. "Family Accommodation in Obsessive-Compulsive Symptoms: Instrument Development and Assessment of Family Behavior." *Journal of Nervous and Mental Disease* 187: 636–42.

Cooper, M. 1996. "Obsessive Compulsive Disorder: Effects on Family Members." *American Journal of Orthopsychiatry* 66: 296–304.

Dindia, K. 2000. "Sex Differences in Self-Disclosure, Reciprocity of Self-Disclosure, and Self-Disclosure and Liking: Three Meta-Analyses Reviewed." In *Balancing the Secrets of Private Disclosures*, edited by S. Petronio. Mahwah, NJ: Lawrence Erlbaum.

Hartl, T. L., S. R. Duffany, G. J. Allen, G. Steketee, and R. O. Frost. 2005. "Relationships among Compulsive Hoarding, Trauma and Attention-Deficit/Hyperactivity Disorder." *Behaviour Research and Therapy* 43 (2): 269–76.

Hayes, S. C., and S. Smith. 2005. *Get Out of Your Mind and Into Your Life: The New Acceptance and Commitment Therapy.* Oakland, CA: New Harbinger Publications.

Hayes, S. C., K. Strosahl, and K. Wilson. 1999. *Acceptance and Commitment Therapy: An Experiential Approach to Behavior Change.* New York: The Guilford Press.

MacGregor, P. 1994. "Grief: The Unrecognized Parental Response to Mental Illness in a Child." *Social Work* 39: 160–65.

Magne-Ingvar, U., and A. Öjehagen. 2005. "Significant Others of Persons with Mental Health Problems: The Testing of a Questionnaire on the Burden of Significant Others." *Nordic Journal of Psychiatry* 59 (6): 441–47.

Martell, C. R., S. Dimidjian, and R. Herman-Dunn. 2010. *Behavioral Activation for Depression: A Clinician's Guide.* New York: The Guilford Press.

Marx, M., and J. Cohen-Mansfield. 2003. "Hoarding Behavior in the Elderly: A Comparison between Community-Dwelling Persons and Nursing Home Residents." *International Psychogeriatrics* 15 (3): 289–306.

Olatunji, B. O., B. J. Williams, N. Haslam, J. S. Abramowitz, and D. F. Tolin. 2008. "The Latent Structure of Obsessive-Compulsive Symptoms: A Taxometric Study." *Depression and Anxiety* 25: 956–68. doi:10.1002/da.20387.

Patronek, G. J. 1999. "Hoarding of Animals: An Under-recognized Problem in a Difficult to Study Population." *Public Health Reports* 114 (1): 81–88.

Pennebaker, J. W., J. K. Kiecolt-Glaser, and R. Glaser. 1988. "Disclosure of Traumas and Immune Function: Health Implications for Psychotherapy." *Journal of Consulting and Clinical Psychology* 56 (2): 239–45.

Ramos-Cerqueira, A., A. Torres, R. Torresan, A. Negreiros, and C. Vitorino. 2008. "Emotional Burden in Caregivers of Patients with Obsessive-Compulsive Disorder." *Depression and Anxiety* 25 (12): 1020–27.

Tolin, D., R. Frost, G. Steketee, and K. Fitch. 2008. "Family Burden of Compulsive Hoarding: Results of an Internet Survey." *Behaviour Research and Therapy* 46 (3): 334–44.

Wenk, G. L. 2003. "Neuropathologic Changes in Alzheimer's Disease." *Journal of Clinical Psychiatry* 64 (Suppl. 9): 7–10.

Fugen Neziroglu, PhD, ABBP, ABPP, is a board-certified cognitive and behavior psychologist and leading researcher on anxiety disorders. She is the director at the Bio Behavioral Institute in Great Neck, NY; professor at Hofstra University; clinical professor of psychiatry at New York University; and coauthor of *Overcoming Compulsive Hoarding*. She has appeared numerous times on the TLC television series, Hoarders.

Katharine Donnelly, PhD, is a behavior therapist at the Bio Behavioral Institute in Great Neck, NY. Her areas of interest include behavioral and acceptance-oriented therapies and obsessive-compulsive spectrum behaviors. She is also coauthor of *Overcoming Depersonalization Disorder*, another collaboration with Fugen Neziroglu.

FROM OUR PUBLISHER—

As the publisher at New Harbinger and a clinical psychologist since 1978, I know that emotional problems are best helped with evidence-based therapies. These are the treatments derived from scientific research (randomized controlled trials) that show what works. Whether these treatments are delivered by trained clinicians or found in a self-help book, they are designed to provide you with proven strategies to overcome your problem.

Therapies that aren't evidence-based—whether offered by clinicians or in books—are much less likely to help. In fact, therapies that aren't guided by science may not help you at all. That's why this New Harbinger book is based on scientific evidence that the treatment can relieve emotional pain.

This is important: if this book isn't enough, and you need the help of a skilled therapist, use the following resources to find a clinician trained in the evidence-based protocols appropriate for your problem. And if you need more support—a community that understands what you're going through and can show you ways to cope—resources for that are provided below, as well.

Real help is available for the problems you have been struggling with. The skills you can learn from evidence-based therapies will change your life.

Matthew McKay, PhD
Publisher, New Harbinger Publications

new harbinger
CELEBRATING
40 YEARS

**If you need a therapist, the following organization
can help you find a therapist trained in cognitive behavioral therapy (CBT).**

The Association for Behavioral & Cognitive Therapies (ABCT) Find-a-Therapist service offers a list of therapists schooled in CBT techniques. Therapists listed are licensed professionals who have met the membership requirements of ABCT and who have chosen to appear in the directory.

Please visit www.abct.org and click on *Find a Therapist*.

**For additional support for patients, family, and friends,
please contact the following:**

Anxiety and Depression Association of America (ADAA)

Visit www.adaa.org

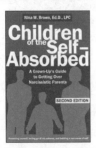